A BARTHOLOMEW MAP & GUIDE

WALK DARTMOOR

35 WALKS SELECTED & DESCRIBED
BY PETER TAVY

JOHN BARTHOLOMEW & SON LTD
EDINBURGH

British Library Cataloguing in Publication Data
Tavy, Peter
    Walk Dartmoor - (A Bartholomew map and guide)
    1. Dartmoor (England) - Description and travel - Guide-books
    I. Title
    914.23′ 5304858   DA670.D2
    ISBN 0-7028-0688-9

First published in Scotland 1984
by John Bartholomew & Son Ltd
Duncan Street, Edinburgh EH9 1TA
Reprinted 1987, 1988

Printed in Scotland
by John Bartholomew & Son Ltd.

The physical landscape of Britain is changing all the time
e.g. as new tracks are made, hedges grubbed up and fields
amalgamated. While every care has been taken in the
preparation of this guide, John Bartholomew & Son Ltd.
will not be responsible for any loss, damage or
inconvenience caused by inaccuracies.

ISBN 0 7028 0688 9

CONTENTS

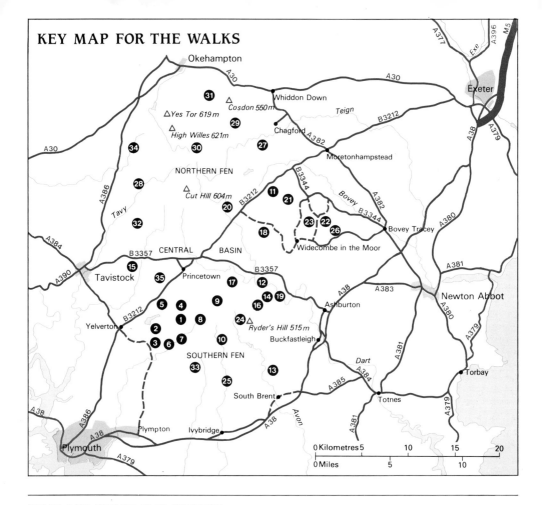

KEY MAP FOR THE WALKS

Okehampton

Whiddon Down

A30

Exeter

③① △ Cosdon 550m
Teign
B3212

△Yes Tor 619m
②⑨ Chagford A382
Moretonhampstead

△ High Willes 621m
③⓪ ②⑦

③④

NORTHERN FEN

②⑧
△ Cut Hill 604m
②⓪ B3212 ①① ②①
Bovey B3344
Bovey Tracey

Tavy
③② ②③②② ②⑥
①⑧ Widecombe in the Moor

B3357 CENTRAL BASIN
①⑤ B3357
Tavistock ③⑤ Princetown ①⑦ ①② A383 Newton Abbot

⑤④ ⑨ ①⑨ Ashburton
①⑥①④
Yelverton ①⑧
②③⑥⑦ ②④△
⑩ Ryder's Hill 515m
Buckfastleigh

SOUTHERN FEN
③③
②⑤ ①③ Dart Torbay

South Brent Totnes

Plympton Ivybridge

Plymouth

| 0 Kilometres | 5 | 10 | 15 | 20 |
| 0 Miles | 5 | 10 | | |

SCALE AND KEY TO MAP SYMBOLS

SCALE 1:40 000   CONTOUR INTERVAL 10m

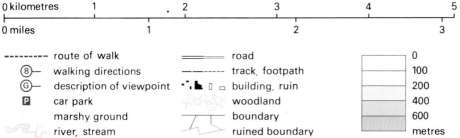

| 0 kilometres | 1 | 2 | 3 | 4 | 5 |
| 0 miles | 1 | 2 | 3 | | |

- - - - - - - - route of walk
⑧— walking directions
Ⓖ— description of viewpoint
🅿 car park
marshy ground
river, stream

road
track, footpath
building, ruin
woodland
boundary
ruined boundary

0
100
200
400
600
metres

1 INTRODUCTION TO DARTMOOR

Everyone has seen imaginary drawings of sea serpents trailing behind them a series of diminishing humps. The granite of South West England resembles the mythical serpent (except that it is headless) in that the upthrust in this region of molten magma from the earth's centre, 290 million years ago, resulted in just such a serpentine series of diminishing granite humps. The process of cooling and remelting occupied a long period of time. The cupolas or domes of granite rose above their common base - the humps above the serpent's hollows, as it were - to their greatest mass and height to form the Dartmoor granite. This fantastic serpent was almost 200 miles (320 km) long, its headless beginning near Exeter and its tail far out in the Atlantic Ocean west of Lands End.

This immense cupola had its peaks and valleys which suffered weathering and erosion until, at the onset of the intermittent glacial periods, peaks were demolished and valleys deeply excavated. We now live in an 'interglacial', and following the recession of the last ice sheets nearly 13 000 years ago, vegetation began to form, fauna to be established and a carpet of grasses, plants and trees to form such as we now associate with moors and heathlands.

When men first came from their coastal cave-homes to hunt on the upland around 8000 BC, the tors (Celtic - *twr*, a tower) would have been of daunting magnitude; by the time the first settlers arrived, around 2000 BC, topographical proportions were reduced almost to what we see today.

Shape and distinctive features

Dartmoor is a vast oval with a bulge on the northeast side. There are three main topographical areas, the northern and southern fens (areas of peat blanket-bog) and the central basin (central oasis-depression drained by the River Dart and tributaries). The perimeter of the Moor is sharply defined by an escarpment of vary-ing steepness. The overall dimensions are about 30 miles (48 km) from north to south, and 17 miles (27 km) from east to west.

Perhaps most characteristic of this great upland are the granite tors and their clitters - the extensive rockfields below the tors consisting of their debris; the huge depression of the central basin (most highland regions have a central *apex*); the swift and beautiful rivers and the gorges through which they leave the Moor; and the long, sweeping ridges. Notable, too, are the four medieval monasteries (one, Buckfast, revived today) around the south foot of the Moor, the innumerable remains of prehistoric occupation and burial monuments, and the highly unusual relics of medieval longhouses, most of them stricken by the Black Death of 1348.

Dartmoor today

Agriculture and industry, military training and other forms of development and land-use compete severely with conservation and recreational interests on a battle-ground of oscillating outcome. Even recreational demand is in itself so intense as literally to wear away the moor in places such as 'honey-pot' river banks and tors of easy access near the Moor's edge. It would help greatly to preserve the character of the terrain if motoring readers of this guide would observe conscientiously the 'No Vehicles beyond this point' notices, would take their refuse away with them, would desist from attracting ponies onto the roads by feeding them and would, when walking, observe the Country Code. Remember too, that many Devon lanes are deep, steep and narrow, and drivers venturing into them should be as competent to drive backwards as forwards!

An upland of such aloofness and so highly charged with atmosphere as Dartmoor, is inevitably rich in legendary lore, and has cradled crafts, place-names and customs kept alive to this day by an indigenous respect for tradition. These include such activities as building with granite, making 'scrumpy' (rough cider), riding the pony drifts (galloping at speed over the Moor to gather wild ponies) and sheep and cattle herding on horseback, in which women of the moor take part alongside the men. The Dartmoor dialect too, enshrines place-names based on Saxon and even Celtic roots.

Dartmoor's geological wealth

The thermal complexities governing the cooling of the granite created rich mineral veins. Tin occurs on the high moorland; Iron and Copper successively on the perimeter and in the border-country. Following a history covering many centuries, mining in the Dartmoor country ceased before World War II. Peat, formed by decaying vegetation, has also been cut, transported and marketed since the Middle Ages; as time went on its use became chiefly as industrial fuel and for the home hearth. China Clay, another substance resulting from the chemical change caused by decay - this time of the granite - is itself now a huge industry on the granite moors of Devon and Cornwall. Granite quarried from the heart of the tors was exported for almost two centuries until recent years, much of it going into some of London's most important buildings.

2 DARTMOOR AS A NATIONAL PARK

The Moor and its border-country formed one of England's first National Parks and was designated on 30 October 1951. The headquarter offices of the Park authority are at Parke, Bovey Tracey, Devon TQ13 9JQ, and the telephone number is Bovey Tracey 832093 (open Monday-Friday 0900-1700 hrs). Dartmoor National Park Information Centres are found at Princetown, Postbridge, Holne New Bridge, Steps Bridge (Teign Valley), Okehampton, Tavistock and Parke, Bovey Tracey.

Forest of Dartmoor

The Duchy of Cornwall - HRH Prince Charles, The Prince of Wales is the present holder of the dukedom -has since 1337 owned the central area of Dartmoor (56 000 acres/22 663 ha). It includes the three main topographical areas detailed above. The term 'Forest' here does not indicate dense woodland, but the hunting ground of the Sovereign or his heir.

The Moormen

The Moor by shape and character, encourages stock to roam over wide areas rather than use small, localised areas. This necessitates close mutual cooperation between the moorland farmers - the moormen, the true sons of the soil. Some moormen's farms are on the edge of the high moor, some in the central basin, others in the high border-country near the moorgates, so being a skilful horseman is essential to the moorman's work.

3 WALKING SAFELY

Equipment

For adults, well greased boots are better than shoes and jeans better than shorts or skirts. A small unframed rucksack for carrying picnic meals and spare clothing leaves both hands free. The lighter bodyweight and agility of children will effectively modify these recommendations. Everybody however, should always take a woollen garment and a light anorak, even in summer. Cloud-cover and the inevitable accompanying breeze can drastically lower the temperature; if cloud becomes thick enough, drizzle and mist can result at over 1000ft. (305m).

Water flowing over granite is self-purifying. If there are no houses nearby and no dead animal is lying in or near the water for 100 yards (91m) carrying heavy drink containers can be avoided by taking only cordial and diluting it with stream water. It is wise to carry an emergency pack of chocolate and apples if a long walk is planned. Also to wear a brightly coloured outer garment easily seen from a distance or from the air. In the event of an accident and assuming someone can reach a telephone The Dartmoor Rescue Service can be summoned by a 999 telephone call.

If any member of the party suffers a cut, look for sphagnum moss and wash the wound liberally with it. A wound cleaned with sphagnum moss will not turn septic.

Before setting out always tell someone where you plan to go.

Military live-firing exercises

There are three ranges on north Dartmoor. No firing takes place during the month of August; firing at other times is advertised in advance in the *Western Morning News* and in the local newspapers published in the border towns, as well as appearing in Post Offices and Dartmoor Information Centres. Red flags flown on tor and hill summits show that a range is in use; red-and-white striped warning posts indicate the limit of safe approach to a range area in use and *must never be disregarded. Refrain from picking up any metal objects in or near a firing range.* Walks in this guide which enter the ranges are 28, 30, 31 and 32.

Dartmoor's weather

Poised as it is on the South West peninsula at over 2000ft (610m) between two seas, Dartmoor has an oceanic climate, with heavy rainfall, high incidence of mist and strong winds. No walker should underestimate the odds against him if he chooses to ignore signs of such conditions. Walks in the guide that entail crossing large spaces of trackless moorland include a warning about the dangers of mist. If however you are overtaken by mist when crossing a tract of open moor, do not go on but try to retrace your steps and return to the start. To become lost and wander aimlessly in circles can be demoralising and exhausting - especially for children. It can be dangerous in the vicinity of a large mire.

Rivers attain to flood conditions during torrential rain more quickly than those of other British highland regions. To venture out in such weather is actually to watch the developing phenomenon of spate. A river in spate is exceedingly dangerous to man and beast.

The Country Code

1 Guard against all risk of fire
2 Fasten all gates
3 Keep dogs under proper control
4 Keep to the paths across farmland
5 Avoid damaging fences, hedges and walls
6 Leave no litter - take it home
7 Safeguard water supplies
8 Protect wildlife, wild plants and trees
9 Go carefully on country roads
10 Respect the life of the countryside

4 MAP READING

A map is a representation, on flat paper, of the three-dimensional features of the earth. Some boast that given an one inch to the mile (1:63360) map of some strange country they can scan a part of it, and have a mental picture of the landscape it represents. This is possibly an exaggeration. The map certainly details the bones of the landscape; the flesh is left to the imagination. As a map has severe spatial and dimensional limitations it is necessary to interpret. This needs practice. Usually a family walking party has one good map reader and that task is left to him or her. this is unwise; everyone should have a turn! Map reading is important as it is the key to enjoying the countryside. Anyone who lacks this easily acquired skill is denied an essential freedom.

The map's key and the scale are detailed at its base. A brief study is necessary. Once the key features of roads, footpaths, watercourses and hills have been learned you should not get lost. One of the most common mistakes to make when map reading is the wrong identification of the point where you are standing. The path or road is identifiable but the precise place is not. The problem can be solved by correct orientation of the map; that is place the map so that the top is towards the north. The easiest way to do this is to place a compass on it with the north point on the compass card pointing to the top. The map, compass card and the map reader (if he is to avoid reading it sideways or upside down) should all be turned until the compass needle points to magnetic north, which is currently eight degrees to the west of north (352 degrees on the scale). Once the map is orientated, some of the visible physical features can be identified and then with the aid of the map your position in relation to them fixed. Another way to orientate a map without a compass is to turn it until some identifiable feature in the landscape (*eg* a tor) is lined up with the map, then all the other features should fit into place.

Orientation is particularly useful at a viewpoint when you are trying to identify distant features, such as hill or tors.

Walking on Dartmoor is very time-consuming due to constant changes in terrain - clean turf, young grass, grassy tufts, rocks, mires - soft wet, peaty ground - and due allowance should be made for this, as well as for undulations and strong winds, when calculating the probable time needed for a walk. You should also consider the time taken to inspect historical features, which are far more numerous than in other British highland regions. As a general guide allow 35-45 minutes for each mile to be covered.

5 PUBLIC RIGHTS OF WAY

On Dartmoor public rights of way extend over open moorland, sometimes on recognisable paths and tracks but often over unmarked ground. They also exist where there is a notice announcing 'Footpath', 'Public Footpath' or 'Bridle Path'.

Permitted paths and access by traditional let exist through newtakes enclosed by broken walls or by maintained walls with unlocked gates. But it should be clear that much of the land is privately owned and some of the valley is enclosed.

Access to common land: the Forest of Dartmoor, the commons of Devon and a scatter of memorial commons (together covering 41% of the National Park), comprise most of the unenclosed land. The Dartmoor Commons Act, 1985, legalises public access to common land in the National Park and makes provision for byelaws to regulate public behaviour.

6 FLORA AND FAUNA

Animals

Animals encountered on open moorland will be harmless, including bullocks (emasculated bulls). But to enter illegally an enclosed and barred newtake by climbing a wall may bring you face to face with a Red Devon Bull, which is large and uncertain of temper. Dogs must be strictly controlled and not allowed to run free at calving or lambing time. It is wise also to keep a dog at heel on hot still summer days when flies make cattle fractious. Make no attempt to feed ponies, whether you are walking or travelling by car. Badger and otter are rarely seen unless one is alone, dogless, and absolutely silent, and the occasional red fox may cross your path. The grass snake is harmless, but not so the adder; he is identified by the zip-fastener marking on his back. Do not attack him, simply let him go.

Flora

There is an abundance of delicate plant growth; rushes and grasses, mosses and lichens exist in many varieties. Three main types of heather appear on the Moor - ling, bell-heather and cross-leaved heath. Whortleberry plants offer you their luscious black fruit in late summer - they are called bilberries or blueberries in other parts of Britain - and the largest blackberries you are ever likely to have seen, grow for the picking in our border-country lanes. The yellow heads of tormentil appear everywhere; ladies bedstraw on the other hand likes dry soil while the delicate ivy-leafed bell flower grows only in damp conditions.

Birds and insects

The buzzard is the largest bird of prey and identifiable by its remarkable powers of soaring flight. The smaller hawks with a quick wing-beat and hover are kestrels and sparrow hawks. Raven, by no means uncommon, has a slow, heavy wing-beat and emits a 'prk-prk' croak, more guttural than the cawing of carrion crows and rooks. The wheatear 'clacks' away on boulders, the dipper patrols his selected beat up and down the streams, and the heron fishes where he fancies. The skylark is ubiquitous and the cuckoo calls amid the tors in May and June.

Insects are legion. Even the Scottish highland midge is found on Dartmoor, eager to wreck the joys of an evening riverside picnic. Webless black spiders scurry everywhere in the grass, black slugs (which, of course, are not insects) appear in armies after rain, and gorgeous dragonflies gladden one's heart on the stream banks in summer. Honey bees gather heather pollen in summer in the central basin, most of the hives being the property of Buckfast Abbey. The most striking of the caterpillars, and quite common, is that of the Emperor Moth, with green body segments marked by black rings and orange knobs from which bristles protrude.

7 GLOSSARY OF DARTMOOR TERMS

Adit horizontal tunnel driven by miners to drain a mine-working, or provide access to a vertical shaft.

Ancient Tenement A farm in the central basin established in Norman times (or earlier, with rights of turbary and pasture in return for stock-ranger duties performed for the lord of the soil.

Blowing house medieval workshop for processing tin-ore. The remains of some today contain relics of furnace, water-wheel pit, drop-stamps mortar stones, and mould stones in which tin ingots were cast.

Bond-stone a boundary stone, sometimes unmarked, sometimes inscribed with initials of parish or land-owner.

Bronze Age period of pre-history c 1950-500 BC.

Bury artificial mound built for the colonising of rabbits on a warren.

Cleave valley with steep sides, a gorge.

Clitter scattered rockfield below a ruined tor, ice-transported during the Ice Age.

Combe a valley closed at one end.

Cornditch ditch dug on outer side of enclosure wall, the earth being thrown behind the wall to create a bank. Thus deer could not jump into the enclosure but any that entered through an open gate could leap outwards. In short, a ditch to protect the corn.

Cross, granite, medieval rough-hewn from solid granite by monks and erected by them to function as Christian way-marks.

Dolmen Neolithic (*ie* pre-Bronze Age) burial chamber built with large stone uprights and a slab roof.

Featherbed (i) see 'Granite bedding'; (ii) a mire that undulates when trodden on.

Fen The peat bog areas of north and south Dartmoor.

Field system a prehistoric field-plan marked out by reaves.

Gert a deep cutting made by miners to reach a vein of tin.

Granite bedding a solid granite platform, often found on tor summits and in river beds.

Gulf see 'Gert'.

Hole a small gorge.

Hut circle circular stone remains of prehistoric dwelling, originally thatched.

Iron Age period of pre-history *c* 500 BC - 50 AD.

Kistvaen a stone chest for burial of human remains in the Bronze Age, usually by cremation.

Lake a tributary stream of which the source, drained by tinners, was once a tarn.

Leat artificial channel contouring hillsides to carry water by gravity.

Logan stone a rock pivoted upon another at a fine point of balance caused by weathering, and capable of being rocked.

Longhouse traditional Devon farmhouse with central passage dividing human from animal quarters. Many medieval longhouse ruins remain on Dartmoor, most emptied by the Black Death in 1348.

Menhir Celtic - a tall stone; prehistoric monument usually associated with burial.

Mire a valley swamp.

Moorgate access gate to open moor at head of border-country lane.

Mortar stone see 'Blowing house'.

Newtake land taken in from open moorland.

Pound enclosure for animals, usually circular.

Reave a boundary bank of earth and stone; some are prehistoric, some medieval.

Retaining circle circle of small set stones surrounding a Bronze Age interment.

Rock basin natural hollow produced on tors by weathering, and in rivers by erosion.

Slotted gateposts granite posts slotted to 'receive lateral poles, precursor of the hinged gate.

Stannary (Latin *Stanum* - Tin) the highly organised medieval tin industry of Dartmoor.

Stone circle open-air temple of the Bronze Age.

Stone row monumental row of set stones leading from a Bronze Age interment to a terminal stone. The longest known in the world, two and a half miles (4 km) in length, is in the Erme valley on southern Dartmoor.

Tare and feather method of cutting granite after *c* 1800 by inserting punches (tares) into pre-drilled holes, kept in position by tiny iron blades (feathers) and hammering on the tares.

Tinner a medieval worker in tin.

Tinners' house medieval tinners' work-a-week shelter: a tiny house with wolf-proof cupboard and fireplace.

Tor (also Rock) Celtic *Twr*, Cornish *Towr* a rockpile; most have been ruined by Ice Age conditions and weathered in vertical partings and horizontal jointings.

Vermin trap, granite miniature granite tunnel, built and sited by warreners to protect buries from predators. The tunnel had a false floor which, when trodden on, released slate shutters imprisoning the animal.

Warren a rabbit farm; some are of medieval foundation, Ditsworthy and Trowlesworthy on southern Dartmoor being the oldest. Sporting warrens were established by landowners for sport and for replenishing their larders.

Waste a term peculiar to south Dartmoor. It indicates a former open tract of moorland, later enclosed.

DOWN TOR, HINGSTON HILL
4½ miles (7.2 km) Rough and rocky in places

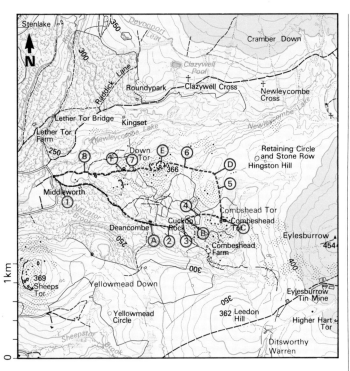

A notable feature of many Dartmoor tributary valleys - other than those in the fen areas - is a pastoral character and a spaciousness that long ago encouraged farming settlers. The Narrator and Newleycombe valleys, tributaries of the River Mewy, are good examples. The valley sides are crested by large tors and clitters, providing an abundance of building stone, and timber was at hand in the woodlands that once extended much further up the valleys than now. The scenery resulting from this unusual topographical pattern today provides pleasure for riders and walkers alike; especially does this apply to the valleys named above - visited yearly by thousands of people and described in this walk.

Drive across Burrator dam and continue for one and a half miles (2.4 km), turning left at a junction, to an official car park, right.

1 *Follow a walled lane, right (Middleworth Lane); pass the ruins of Middleworth Farm - where Middleworth Tor is glimpsed rising boldly above the trees, left - and continue to Deancombe Farm (also ruins), where rick staddles remain beside the track.*

A Ahead lies the fascinating medieval settlement of Deancombe. The rugged lane to the moor (left) passes an old mining adit, and the ruins of 19th century Deancombe Farm lie ahead. Middleworth and Deancombe were two of the many sheep farms that ceased to work after Burrator reservoir was opened in 1898. The initials 'ML' on door lintels indicate ownership by the Massey Lopes family, Sir Massey Lopes later being created Lord Roborough.

2 *Beyond Deancombe, the track leads to a slotted gatepost: from here the bulk of Cuckoo Rock looms ahead. Three more gateways follow.*

3 *Follow the track towards Cuckoo Rock and take a left-fork path climbing steeply between boulders.*

B Cuckoo Rock is the hard-core remnant of a former tor amid a wild profusion of granite, bracken, old grey walls and faded tracks. Tradition recounts the use by 18th century smugglers of several caches in this secluded valley, one at the base of Cuckoo Rock and others nearby. The remains of Combeshead Farm are seen near the stream, Combeshead Brook; this changes its name with each locality, so that Combeshead Brook is succeeded by Deancombe Brook and Narrator Brook (after another abandoned farm near the reservoir). From Cuckoo Rock are seen Sheeps Tor and the nearby rugged piles of Combeshead and Down Tors, while further to the southeast, in contrasting smooth outline, the Plym ridge is etched on the skyline.

4 *Climb northeast from Cuckoo Rock*

Over

and Combeshead Tor will come fully into view. Ancient crudely built boulder-walls lie on the hillside.

C Combeshead Tor is a widespread ruin. Lether and Sharp Tors rise in the west above the waters of Burrator, while higher and more distant tors appear in the north-east. Between the tor and dominant Eylesburrow is the high, wide head-valley, completely worked out by tinners, of Combeshead Brook. In the near distance is Down Tor and, intermediately, Hingston Hill, its dome covered by a scattering of small rocks.

5 *Pass through an unfinished stone wall and approach the head (left) of a stone row visible on the plain; the tips of a stone circle (left) appear as you walk.*

D The Hingston Hill stone row and retaining circle were restored in 1880 by the Revd Sabine Baring-Gould and Robert Burnard. The single row ends at a blocking stone,

and the retaining circle once contained a kistvaen. The whole scene, a fine monument in a wild setting, provides an atmospheric link with prehistory typical of Dartmoor.

6 *Walk north-west for 60 yds (55 m) to a prominent cairn from where Down Tor is visible. Walk direct to the tor and ascend its north side.*

E Down Tor. Visible from the summit are 23 tors and countless hills; progressively nearer are Burrator Lake, the ancient enclosure walls of Deancombe Farm and a vast clitter containing many huge rocks.

7 *Descend westward from the tor, keeping the lake slightly to your left. A path appears below passing through a broken wall to the scattered pile of Deancombe Rocks. Turn and regard the cone and clitter of Down Tor, an astonishing wilderness of granite indicating its former gigantic proportions. Pass Deancombe Rocks and (in summer when the bracken is high) follow a well-worn path.*

CAUTION: *adders bask here in high summer and badger setts and fox earths mean concealed holes. The sound of Newleycombe Lake is audible as you follow the path to the next rockpile.*

F Middleworth Tor has a pillar formation caused by giant frost-partings in the rock. A basin has formed on the summit and another below: the ruined Middleworth Farm is seen in the valley and Lether Tor appears from here at its most impressive.

8 *Continue westward from the tor, cross the head of the Middleworth packhorse lane (from farm to common) and make for a small rockpile shaded by trees; this is Snappers Tor, with two basins on the summit. The continuing path is overgrown, but becomes clear at an old wall on the west side of the tor. Open ground follows on the foot of the ridge and the car park is visible below.*

SHEEPS TOR AND YELLOWMEAD CIRCLE

3 miles (4.8 km) Easy; gradual climb of 450 ft (137 m); dry

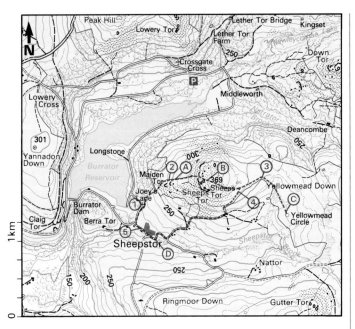

The area of south-west Dartmoor surrounding Burrator Lake and the huge pile of Sheeps Tor contains some of the most beautiful scenery in southern England. The lake, a Plymouth Corporation reservoir (now South West Water Authority) occupies the bed of a primeval lake, its shores overlooked by the fine tors of Sharp, Lowery, Lether, Down and the greatest of them, Sheeps. The name 'Sheeps' is a corruption of the medieval 'Schittes' - a steep slope. Both the valley and village at its south foot take its name. Drive across Burrator dam and take the first turning left at a junction. Park at the top of a slight rise in the lane, where ample space exists.

1 *Walk up Joey's Lane, right, an ancient packhorse way on 'featherbed' granite; pass through an old gateway; a nearby stone inscribed 'PCWW' indicates Plymouth Corporation Water Works boundary ie, Burrator catchment area. Climb the steep green path ahead to a broken rockpile.*

2 *Maiden Tor. A low outcrop on the massif of Sheeps Tor. Several long mounds here, pitted with holes, were the breeding 'buries' of an old rabbit warren.*

A Viewpoint: beyond the lake is seen the line of the former Great Western Railway Princetown line threading the plantations on Yannadon; to the right are Sharp and Lether Tors rising on the right.

B Sheeps Tor. Ease the climb by zigzagging. The greatest of the summit piles is at the south-east corner, where the sheer rockface is used by Royal Marine Commandos for practice-climbs. A system of low funnel walls near the brink (another lies at the foot of the rockface) is the relic of a warren vermin trap. Notice the stones of Yellowmead Circle distant on the down, and the long, undulating ridges of southern Dartmoor in the south-east.

3 *Make due east for the newtake corner; follow the wall, right; continue to the circle.*

C This is a rare fourfold concentric circle of the early Bronze Age, the only other example on Dartmoor being on Shoveldon in North Teign country (Walk 29). Within the innermost circle is the hollow where once the burial kistvaen lay.

4 *Return to the newtake corner (Note 3); follow the wall south-west for 600 yds (549 m) to the next corner. Turn with it and descend to the head of Tor Lane; follow this to the village.*

D In the churchyard wall opposite a cottage (near the village centre) is St Leonard's Well, its canopy a medieval window-tracery taken from the church. Take the footpath nearby into the churchyard and see the granite tombs of three 19th century Rajahs of Sarawak. This beautiful little Dartmoor church has pillars of granite hewn from the clitter of the huge tor above.

5 *Leave the churchyard by the lych gate, follow the road, right, and return to the start.*

Walk 3

BURRATOR GORGE AND MEAVY VALLEY

2¾ miles (4.4 km) Very easy; muddy after rain

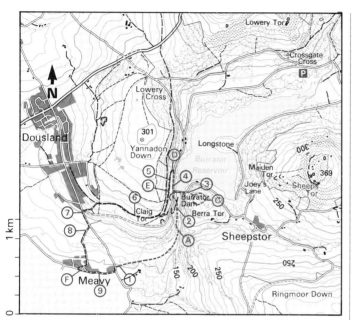

features in the valley. Its mighty slabs are cast about the hill below in spectacular fashion.

4 *Re-cross the dam; turn right; walk for 200 yds (183 m).*

D Above the left (west) roadside in a wooded glade is the cascading outflow of another leat - the Devonport, built in 1794.

5 *From the glade, follow a track, left, up the hillside to the site of Burrator Halt on the former GWR Yelverton-Princetown railway (closed 1956).*

E The view from the halt includes: Sharp, Lether and Down Tors, and Sheepstor village and church nestling beneath the brow of the great tor above.

6 *Follow the rail track around the south spur of Yannadon. The Burrator-Dousland road and the Plymouth leat are below while above is the Devonport (see also Walk 5). Leave the railroad at a curve and descend (left) to the cattle grid and road junction below.*

7 *The Plymouth leat passes beneath the Dousland road. Follow the Meavy road downhill for 200 yds (183 m) to a junction.*

8 *Turn right into Rectory Lane; pass the rectory gate, enter Meavy village centre at the Green.*

F The medieval church, rebuilt in the 15th century, was dedicated to St. Peter and consecrated in the year 1122. The Church House has become the Royal Oak Inn, its name derived from the celebrated, ancient relic outside its front door; under its branches is held the annual Meavy Oak Fair in June.

9 *Follow the road eastward through the village to reach the start.*

This walk passes through a very attractive piece of south west Dartmoor borderland and involves very little climbing. The ancient name of the river dammed at Burrator to supply Plymouth's water is Mew or Mewy. Its fine lower reach is easily accessible. Park at the roadside opposite Meavy School at the east end of the village.

1 *Walk through the gateway beside the old smithy (now called 'Moor View') and follow the woodland path, which crosses the former Meavy mill leat.*

A Sheepstor Brook joins the river in the gorge and the massive granite wall of the dam is seen through the trees. The remains of the mill-leat weir are below, and on the hillside above the path, left, is the dry channel of the historic Plymouth leat, built by Sir Francis Drake in 1589 to carry drinking water to the city of Plymouth.

2 *Follow the path up to the leat, and then to the road above. Turn right, cross the dam and enjoy the prospect of the tors reflected in the lake.*

B The reservoir (completed 1898) made the Plymouth leat redundant. Conspicuous heights above the lake's further shore extend from Peak Hill to Cramber Down.

3 *At the east end of the dam, mount a flight of steps (right) and follow a steep path (left) to a rockpile.*

C Berra Tor ('beara' - a wood, the tor in the wood) gives its name in the form 'Burrator' to several

13

CLAZYWELL POOL, CRAMBER POOL, LETHER TOR BRIDGE

5½ miles (8.8 km) Moderately easy

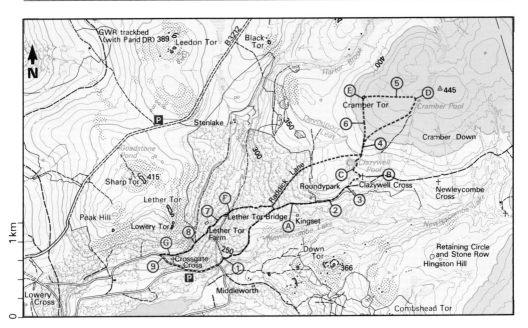

Moorland tarns were once numerous on Dartmoor, but the medieval tinners, wishing to explore the tarn-beds for tin-stone deposits, took steps to drain almost all of them. Thus we are left with what man has created in their place - water-filled mining pits; these are sometimes sinister, sometimes beautiful, but never commonplace. One example each of the sinister and the beautiful is incluoed in this walk.

Drive across Burrator dam and continue for one and a third miles (2.1 km); take the first turning left at a junction; drive to a car park (right) situated near the head of the reservoir.

1 *Follow the stony track rising eastward; the green plateau above the car park is the site of old Norsworthy Farm.*

Continue up the track (Norsworthy Lane); notice a large boulder (right) in which are embedded some mason's tares and feathers. The ascending lane affords pleasing views across the Newleycombe Lake valley

A An old gateway (right) gives access to the ruined Kingset Farm and a fine view of rugged Down Tor.

2 *Continue up the main track through a gateway (Cockles Gate) to a point opposite the remains of Clazywell Farm, where a deep gert come down to the track from the hillside, left.*

3 *Leave the track, walk up the edge of the gert to the granite cross, right.*

B Clazywell Cross is one of the series of medieval crosses marking the trans-Dartmoor monastic route between the abbeys of Buckfast (east) and Tavistock (west).

C Clazywell Pool, an old mine working, is described in legend as bottomless, apparently on the strength of a sounding taken long ago by tying together the bell ropes of Walkhampton Church and lowering a bell into its depths; when the ropes were paid out, still the submerged bell rang! Dartmoor explorer Robert Burnard, using a more scientific approach a century ago, found the greatest depth to be 20 ft (6 m).

4 *Follow a well-defined path north to Clazywell Bridge over the Devonport leat, here quite near its cascade on Raddick Hill (See Walk 5, note 4). Now bear right (north-east) and climb the flank of Cramber Down to another gert (Cramber Gert) running up the hill and leading to -   Over*

D Cramber Pool. This little known tarn is far more attractive than the much visited Clazywell Pool below, being fringed with bog plants and mosses that colour its seclusion delightfully in spring and summer. Views are rewarding and almost identical to those seen from Cramber Tor (Note E).

5 *Walk due west along the ridge of Cramber Down towards the south shoulder of Leedon Hill (with the grotesque Leedon Tor on its north shoulder) to reach a small rockpile ahead, below the crest of the ridge.*

E Cramber Tor is a much broken pile. Take time to absorb the fine view (due rather to the tor's position on the hill-spur than its elevation): Cornwall's Bodmin Moor appears between Dartmoor's western tors; sunshine catches the rippling waters of Plymouth Sound; the Plym ridge rises in the south, with Hen Tor overlooked by Shiel Top. In the north, beyond the tower of Princetown church, Great Links Tor and the domes of Amicombe and Cut Hills rise to almost 2000 ft (610 m).

6 *Walk south to re-cross Clazywell Bridge. Bear right (south-west) towards the plantations and enter the gateway to Raddick Lane, which descends through the trees to the river, and joins a riverside track leading to a clapper bridge with parapets, steps and ford.*

F Lether Tor Bridge, the last of its type built on Dartmoor, cost £12.10s in 1833! It has survived to carry modern forestry vehicles.

7 *Beyond the bridge, the track passes the entrance to a large cache: this was used in turn by smugglers, and farmers of nearby Lether Tor Farm; the scant remains of the old farm are nearby, right of the track.*

8 *Continue past the farm; re-cross the Devonport leat and stop at the junction of the track with a tarmac road.*

G Here, under the shadow of the plantations' outer trees, and on the further bank of the leat, stands the headless Lowery Cross, another mark on the monastic way, though the only remaining original portions are the arms and base. The tor nearest here, spreading a considerable clitter on the hillside above, is Lowery Tor, a satellite pile of Lether Tor.

9 *Turn left into the road and descend the hill, passing between the old enclosures of Lether Tor Farm (left) and Vinneylake Farm (right). At the foot of the hill is the junction with the reservoir perimiter road; 500 yds (457 m) beyond it you will re-cross Mewy and be back at the start.*

15

Walk 5
BLACK TOR and the UPPER MEWY VALLEY
2½ miles (4 km) Easy; dry

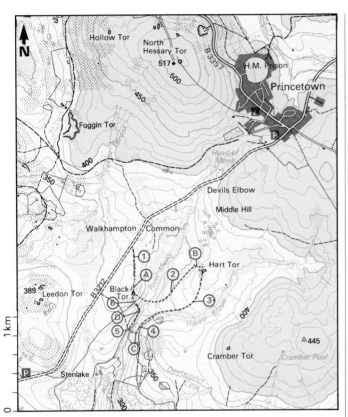

burial cairn. Each cairn has a retaining circle. Climb to Hart Tor.

B The tor heads a considerable clitter and has a large area of granite bedding on the summit. The river disappears southwards below conifer-clad hillsides between Lether and Sheeps Tors and the stream flowing around the east/south foot of the tor takes its name - Hartor Brook.

3 *Follow the brook downstream to an enclosed Bronze Age village; the pound entrance retains the original paving and the huts have protective entrance passages, once roofed.*

4 *Walk downstream to see the cascading Devonport leat on Raddick Hill, and aqueducted across the River Mewy - a delightful spot known as Iron Bridge.*

5 *Cross the river and walk upstream past the numerous pits and mounds left by medieval tinners, to reach Black Tor Hole.*

D Central in the dell is a twisting waterfall beneath rowan trees where Mewy creates a deep pool. On both river banks is the ruin of a blowing house, each in use until the mid-17th century, the tin processed here being marketed in the stannary town of Tavistock. Each house contains mortar stones, and its leat from the river is traceable. On the remaining door-lintel of the left bank house is inscribed the Roman numeral 'XIII' (13), being the registered number in stannary records of the house.

6 *A zigzag path leads from the dell to the tor above; follow this to the start. Notice as you walk the weird outline of Leedon Tor three quarters of a mile (1.2 km) to the west.*

This attractive piece of country near Princetown is easily reached. Take the Yelverton-Princetown road (B3212) for one and a half miles (2.4 km) beyond Goadstone Pond, a small sheet of water (right) on the crest of the moorland escarpment. Parking space may be found on either side of the road.

1 *Follow the clear path from the parking space to the tor, which rises due south of the road.*

A Black Tor has two piles; at the smaller is a huge logan stone pivoted on its base; it could be rocked until recent years: a large pear-shaped basin lies on its upper face. The larger pile has a rockface on its east side, and an interior rock-chimney. Descend to the valley, cross the River Mewy at Black Tor Ford and make for the stone rows ahead.

2 *On the left (east) bank a double row leads to a burial cairn at the foot of Hart Tor; parallel to it, a much ruined single row also leads to a*

RINGMOOR DOWN ANTIQUITIES, LEGIS TOR
3 miles (4.8 km) Very easy

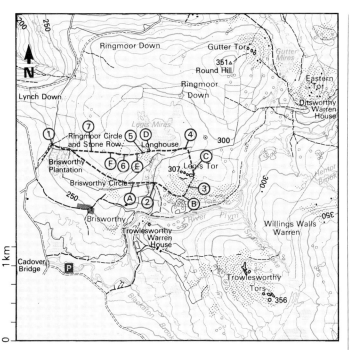

The smooth terrain of Ringmoor Down offers easy walking; reached either from the Meavy-Sheepstor or Meavy-Cadover Bridge roads, it gives good views over Mewy and Plym countries. Do not be alarmed by military 'dry-training', (exercises with blank ammunition). Take the Meavy-Cadover Bridge road to Brisworthy Plantation: turn into a track (north side of road) and park near a 'No Vehicles beyond this point' notice.

1 *Follow the plantation wall to the northeast corner; cross the down, keeping Legis Tor to your right. Brisworthy appears below, right, and the Plym ridge rises eastward from*

Shiel Top. Clay workings (right) and Trowslesworthy, formerly a warren house, appear beyond the Plym valley. Pass through a small rockfield and bear towards Legis Tor until a Bronze Age circle appears, right.

A Brisworthy stone circle has 27 erect stones; it is 79 ft (24 m) in diameter and is seen to advantage against the background of Legis Tor.

2 *Follow the track from the circle to Legis Lake Ford; cross; walk ahead to Bronze Age pounds and enclosed hut circles below the tor.*

B The remains occupy a large bracken-free patch and were the homes of the people who practised

their religious rites in Brisworthy circle.

3 *Legis Tor consists of four piles; one or two useable paths (unavoidably through bracken and clitter) lead to the largest.*

C Legis Tor offers an excellent view of the moorland Plym valley. Directly below the main pile (south side) are the funnel walls of an almost perfect vermin trap, while rabbit buries appear beyond.

4 *Walk north for 200 yds (183 m), keeping above the bracken line, to a crumbled wall. Pass through it, descend (left) to Legis Mires Ford just below the source-mire of Legis Lake, where stepping stones remain. Follow the wide track ahead to some overgrown ruins.*

D Here is a 12th/13th century longhouse, with subsidiary buildings, garden and paddock, in an unspoilt setting.

Walk for a short way towards the westward slope terminating the Plym ridge, pass through a small rockfield to a kistvaen.

E A large tilted slab is the coverstone of the kistvaen, which is in perfect condition.

6 *Follow an ancient boundary ditch up the hill to another Bronze Age monument, Ringmoor circle and row; both were restored in recent times. The ditch joins another coming up the hill. Walk parallel to it and another circle appears on the crest of the down; this is a small retaining circle of border-rock and quartzite.*

F View the panorama of east Cornwall beyond the Tamar valley.

7 *Return to the corner of Brisworthy Plantation and the start.*

Walk 7

GUTTER TOR, DITSWORTHY, THRUSHELCOMBE, EYLESBURROW.

5½ miles (8.8 km) Moderately easy

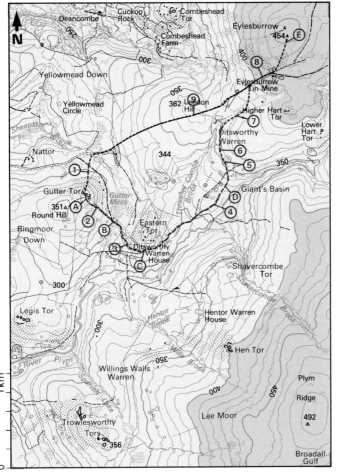

Sheepstor village and Burrator Lake; descend to a road junction, turn right; when opposite the rocks of Gutter Tor (right), park in the space provided near the plank bridge and ford (Burcombe Ford on Sheepstor Brook).

1 *Climb Gutter Tor, keeping the extensive main clitter to your left.*

A Gutter Tor was named after the goats that grazed there when medieval farms below were occupied. On the summit rock are several rock basins, the largest having a drainage channel and lip.

2 *Walk round Cats' Corner, (where wild cats once had their setts) and follow a green path on the south side of the tor descending to the hard track below.*

B A short way below the foot of the main pile (left) and an enormous bedrock (right), are the remnant walls of a vermin trap verging the path, the relic at the intersection being the coverstone drilled to hold the trap-springing mechanism. Beyond the trap (right) are the oblong foundations of a longhouse, and everywhere around, the buries of the huge Ditsworthy Warren. Immediately ahead are the roof and chimneys of the warren house, and beyond them the tall standing stones of Thrushelcombe, wrongly spoken of as 'Drizzlecombe'.

3 *Join the hard track, pass Gutter Mires (source of Sheepstor Brook) and walk among more buries to the warren house.*

C Ditsworthy Warren House is used by Royal Navy cadets and dockyard apprentices for adventure

Over

Southwest Dartmoor contains a rich variety of antiquities in a unique setting; those included in this walk extend over a time period of 3500 years, from early Bronze Age homes and monuments to a tin mine closed in 1852 and a commercial rabbit warren in 1945. NOTE: Eylesburrow Mine, which was worked from 1815-1852, covers an extensive area and is here conveniently divided between Walks 7 and 8. Take the Cornwood road from Meavy village; at the top of Lynch Hill turn left at the Sheepstor signpost. Fork right near a tiny cottage (right), cross the spur of Ringmoor Down and enjoy the view, overlooked by Sheeps Tor, of

training. A hollow on the right near the entrance gate, now by-passed by the leat that once supplied it, was the warren 'carrion pool' where carrion meat was dipped for cleansing before being fed to the warren dogs; these were employed for driving rabbits into the capture nets pegged out near the buries. Pass behind the house and look down into a walled enclosure, right; this was the dog pit ('Kennel court') where the animals had freedom of movement but could not leap the overhanging stone coping - part of which remains today.

4 *Follow the track north-east; above (left) is the clitter of Eastern Tor; below, (right) the River Plym; beyond it, the dark cone of Hen Tor protrudes from the flank of the Plym ridge, and the Thrushelcombe stones are ahead. When the track bends right towards the river, leave it, cross Thrushelcombe Brook and follow a green path to the stones.*

D This sanctuary of the Bronze Age dead is enhanced by an unspoilt environment. Three parallel rows are each headed by a (ruined) grave with retaining circle and terminated by a menhir, the south-east stone (14 ft/4 m high) being the tallest on Dartmoor. Its axe-like head is natural, for no evidence exists that Dartmoor's prehistoric peoples ever shaped their monuments. 'Giants' Basin' is the large burial barrow nearby. On the flank of Thrushelcombe Hill above are the huts of the monument builders.

5 *Walk to the huts and take a closer look.*

6 *Walk to a mound topped by a leaning slab. This exceptionally fine kistvaen is surrounded by remains of the cairn that once covered it.*

7 *Follow the brook upstream. Masonry here and there denotes the fringe of the Eyleburrow Mine complex, the first example being a water-wheel pit and (above left) the bank at the end of the leat from which water was channelled to the wheel. A larger ruin includes some dressed masonry; this was built in 1820 to smelt the tin-ore raised at the mine - which formerly had to be carted to Calenick in Cornwall for smelting.*

8 *Follow the brook upstream to reach the outline of the mine reservoir (now dry), which was fed by a leat from the upper Plym; more wheel-pits appear as you ascend the mine road. Stones standing in pairs beside the road bear rust-stained grooves; these held iron axles supporting oscillating flat-rods for transmitting power from the great wheel (note 9) to mine-shaft pumps near the hilltop.*

E On Eylesburrow's summit are two burial cairns, and an excellent panoramic view over Dartmoor's central basin reaching to the remoter northern heights.

9 *Descend the mine road, pausing to inspect the pit for the great wheel installed in 1847. On the grass mountain of Eylesburrow where a few generations ago, 60 men toiled, now silence reigns. The leat with bridge and causeway at the foot of the hill is ancient, and still carries water from Thrushelcombe Brook to Sheepstor village. The start is visible 300 yds (274 m) ahead.*

Walk 8
PLYM FORD, EYLESBURROW TIN MINE (EAST)
4½ miles (7.2 km) Climbs gradual; some rough ground.

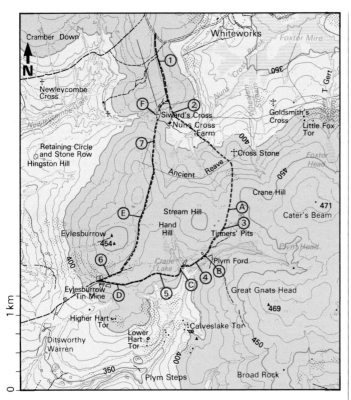

through the newtake at some distance from the house, descending to a bridge over the Devonport leat and a ford on Nuns Cross Brook.

2 *Follow the track beyond the ford and continue towards a prominent boulder on the hill directly ahead. As you go, notice an upright stone away to the left; this bears an incised cross and probably marks an old boundary. Next cross an ancient reave which can be seen curving westward round the hills. Pass to the right of the prominent boulder and choose any path leading (right) towards the upper end of a series of tinners' pits on the shoulder of Stream Hill - the only such pits visible in the locality.*

A Viewpoint: the central basin lies spread in the north, the bold height of Great Gnats Head (crowned by a cairn) appears in the south-east and Eylesburrow, with its two cairns in the west.

3 *As you top the rise the upper Plym valley appears below: make for the place where paths beyond the river are seen to converge on a ford.*

B Plym Ford is set in wild country; a water-wheel pit for a distant working of Eylesburrow Mine has been built in a gert directly above the ford: notice the mouth of the carefully constructed conduit - the 'tail-race' - through which water escaped from the pit, after use, into the gert. The Plym ridge rises in the south; tors and clay works in the south-west mark the river's middle reach, while Plymouth and its Sound provide a background of blue haze.

4 *Follow the mine road south-west,*

This route, which should not be attempted if mist is likely, enables the walker to see that part of the Eylesburrow mine complex not visited in Walk 7. The domed hill of Eylesburrow on the south-west moor provides one of the best possible views over the Dartmoor central basin. It is also on the Forest boundary, and from it are visible other important points on this historic line, such as Great Mis Tor, North and South Hessary Tors, Watern Hill and Ryder. Branch south-east from the B3212 road just below the village square in Princetown. Drive for two and a quarter miles (3.6 km). Stop at the second of two tracks (unsigned) branching right from the road at a point where this descends to the old mining settlement of Whiteworks (below, left). Park - but not on the track.

1 *Follow the rough road to Nuns Cross Farm. This deserted settlement (used now for adventure training) is named from the ancient monument seen outside its west enclosure wall, properly Siward's Cross. Follow a track*

Over

noticing the fine view of the river's upper reach valley, left, beneath the great folds of the southern hills. The rockpile of Lower Hart Tor is especially picturesque.

C The tributary valley ahead is a sylvan spot. Here, a leat from Crane Lake once turned another large water-wheel of the extraordinary Eylesburrow complex (all built and engineered, by men of the 18th century) which operated two sets of ore-crushing stamps.

5 *From the mine road beyond the valley, the mining mounds on Eylesburrow's south flank and the rathr insignificant rocks of Higher Hart Tor appear ahead. Walk to the centre of the mine-buildings area.*

D Ruins on the south side of the mine road include the once dignified house of the mine captain, the smithy, timber and peat stores, gunpowder cellar and counting house (mine office). On the right is the extensive ruin of the 'barracks' - the West Country miners' term for their hostel. Near the latter a branch track comes over the shoulder of the hill, right.

6 *Follow the branch track north-east past several mineshafts: the first of these is still open, revealing its built-up masonry sides, but the others are in-filled. The row of flat-rod stones here shows how near the hill summit power had to be transmitted from the great wheel (see Walk 7, note 8).*

E As the track crests the Eylesburrow-Hand Hill col, note the marvellous sweep of open moorland with, far right, the distant dome of Ryder, south Dartmoor's highest point.

7 *The northward descending track con verges, near the foot of the hill, with a reave, one containing bond-stones at intervals, marking the Forest boundary. Continue to a granite cross ahead.*

F Siward's Cross, a wonderful relic of the Middle Ages, is first mentioned in a document of 1240 as a major point on the Perambulation of the Forest boundary in that year. From here walk round the north-west corner of Nuns Cross Farm Newtake, rejoin the farm road and return to the start.

Walk 9

FOX TOR, CHILDE'S TOMB, WHITEWORKS

4 miles (6.4 km) One easy climb; three river crossings difficult after heavy rain

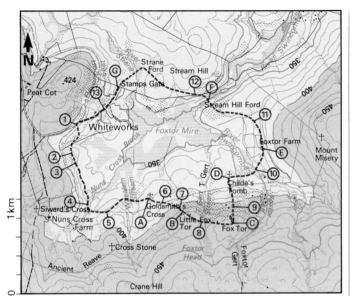

This walk is a circular route around the 'Great Grimpen Mire' of Conan Doyle's *The Hound of the Baskervilles*. Foxtor Mire, its real name, is a vast swamp watered by several streams and drained by the River Swincombe. It is, in fact, the upper reach basin of Swincombe and the scene of a legendary medieval tragedy. Foxtor Mire, at times admittedly sinister in appearance, is lethal near its lower centre and an escaping prisoner from Princetown Prison was swallowed in its depths many years ago.

Branch south-east from the B3212 road just below the village square in Princetown; pass Peat Cot and continue down the hill towards Whiteworks. Park in a disused quarry, left, near the Devonport leat bridge.

1 *Cross the leat and follow the leatside path downstream. Flowing well above the valley floor it gives excellent views across Foxtor Mire. The dark rocks of Fox Tor, below the skyline of Caters Beam, appear in the south-east as the leat flanks Nuns Cross Hill.*

2 *Cross the first broken wall, which descends to the valley; when opposite a huge boulder on the leat's right bank, walk down to inspect the stones of a fine kistvaen and retaining circle below the path (left).*

3 *Regain the leat path; half a mile (0.8 m) onward is the second broken wall, near which stands a small tin hut. Continue to a third wall, which appears just before the leat bends to the right.*

4 *Here leave the leatside path and descend to the valley of Nuns Cross*

Brook. Follow the continuing wall eastward.

5 *On reaching a tributary of Nuns Cross Brook, leave the wall and bear left to an inconspicuous granite cross 300 yds (274 m) north-east. Cross a dry leat channel which once carried water to Whiteworks Mine.*

A Goldsmith's Cross, on the trans-Dartmoor monastic way, was discovered fallen in 1903 by Lieutenant Goldsmith RN, and subsequently set in the bedrock.

6 *Follow a visible path east of the cross. Fox Tor will appear much nearer. with its satellite Little Fox Tor above right.*

7 *Make for Little Fox Tor; it provides the easiest approach to the main tor. Cross the wall of Foxtor Newtake at the foot of the hill wherever convenient.*

B From Little Fox Tor note the extent of the great mire below, and the shape of the central basin beyond, backed by northern Dartmoor. On the east side of this decayed tor is the deep T Gert, containing a tinners' house under its east side.

8 *Keep to the high ground, cross the head of the gert, and walk to -*

C Fox Tor. Dartmoor novelist Eden Phillpotts wrote in his *The American Prisoner*, 'Beneath Caters Beam, and dwarfed thereby, arise the twin turrets of Fox Tor' - the 'twin turrets' being the two largest piles of the tor. At the foot of one, a fallen summit rock has two rock basins. The tor.is peninsulated by T Gert Stream (west) and Foxtor Stream (east) in Foxtor Gulf, on the east. Look

Over

down on the plain of Sand Parks from here to where another monastic cross stands on a plinth. It is approached by a clear path from the hunting gate in the newtake wall below. Also visible (right) are the ruins of lonely Foxtor Farm.

9 *Descend to the hunting gate and walk to the cross.*

D Childes's Tomb. The granite plinth supporting the cross appears, on approach, to be a box-like structure; it is actually the Bronze Age kistvaen (partly restored) in which the corpse of 14th century landowner and huntsman, Amyas Childe of Plymstock was temporarily laid. Completely lost while hunting in a blizzard near the fringe of the mire as night drew near, Childe slew his mare, disembowelled her and crept inside the carcase for warmth. But to no avail, for he froze to death. The whole grisly mass was discovered next day by a moorman,

who gave the alarm and deposited the terrible remains in the kistvaen.

10 *Follow a path to the ruins of Foxtor Farm, crossing the River Swincombe where convenient.*

E Foxtor Farm, a forlorn and lonely ruin, brought little joy to its occupants during a period of tenancy of less than a century after its construction in 1809. It is also featured in Phillpott's *The American Prisoner.*

11 *Walk north-west from the farm, along a path which rounds the upper edge of a wet hollow (left). Now overgrown in places, the path was once in regular use between the farm and Stream Hill Ford on the river.*

F Swincombe will be more difficult to cross at Stream Hill Ford as the waters of Foxtor Mire and Strane River have now joined its course. If necessary, remove boots and wade. The remains of the headweir of the Wheal Emma leat (cut in 1859 to supply a copper mine at West

Buckfastleigh) are beside the ford, and above them the tributary river Strane flows into Swincombe.

12 *Follow the path from a hunting gate (left bank) which contours the spur of Stream Hill and joins the Sherberton-Whiteworks track. Strane Ford is little used now and has marshy approaches. Cross; follow a track (left) to the Whiteworks enclosure.*

G Enter Whiteworks at Stamps Gate, near where an ore-stamping plant once stood. Whiteworks Mine, like Eylesburrow, had become a large-scale mechanised establishment by 1820. South of the tarmac road to Princetown are shafts and tramroad trackbeds; on the north side are ruined cottages and, further up the hill, the mine captain's house.

13 *Passing the highest placed of the houses, continue along the road for 250 yds (229 m) to reach the leat bridge and the start.*

BLACK LANE (SOUTH) AND DUCKSPOOL
6 miles (9.6 km) Some very wet ground after prolonged rain

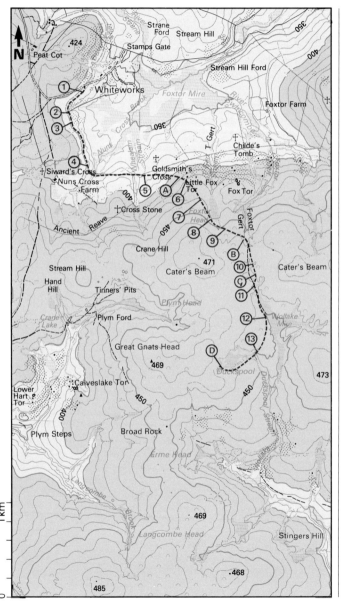

The idea of a hidden receptacle among the hills where explorers may leave their mail, first franking it with a rubber stamp secreted there and bearing the name location, is an old one. On Dartmoor there are three traditional post-boxes - excursions to two of them included in this guide (Walks 10 and 30); the third, Vur Tor on the northern moor, is too remote for easy family walking. Do not forget to take a stamped postcard or envelope with you for the customary franking and deposit.

This walk uses a peat pass through the southern fen known as Black Lane (South), a through-passage for horsemen and herds from southern Dartmoor to the central basin. Its name derives from the rich, black peat which it penetrates. WARNING: this is an out-and-return walk on the same route; do not, if children are present, attempt any kind of short cut to avoid the angular approach to Black Lane, as the terrain of the fen is exhausting. If mist appears likely, do not undertake the walk at all.

Branch south-east from the B3212 road just below the village square in Princetown; pass Peat Cot and continue down the hill towards Whiteworks. Park in a disused quarry, left, near the Devonport leat bridge.

1 *Cross the leat and follow the leatside path downstream.*

2 *Cross the first broken wall, which descends to the valley; when opposite a huge boulder on the leat's right bank, walk down to inspect the stones*

Over

of a fine kistvaen and retaining circle below the path (left).

3 Regain the leat path; half a mile (0.8 km) onward is the second broken wall, near which stands a small tin hut. Continue to the third wall, which appears just before the leat bends to the right.

4 Here leave the path and descend to the valley of Nuns Cross Brook. Cross. Pass through the broken wall and follow it over the low hill ahead and down to the next valley (Whealam Stream). Cross a little way upstream if the ground is wet.

5 The wall now bends left; leave it and continue on its previous alignment to a scattering of rocks on the hill-spur ahead; some convenient paths exist. On the hilltop, check your alignment with the wall.

A Enjoy the view of the central basin.

6 A path leads ahead to a larger rock outcrop - Little Fox Tor. On approach you will see a transverse valley opening up, and a wide shallow basin above it, right. This is T Gert, the basin being the source of T Gert Stream.

7 Follow a clear path round the head of the basin in order to avoid the mire.

8 On leaving the basin notice the rocks of Fox Tor (left) and a deep valley

opening between it and your path: this is Foxtor Head.

9 Your path and Fox Tor are equidistant from the Head: it will lead you to a gert.

B On the west side of the gert is a fine medieval tinner's house; in common with many features in this locality, it bears the name of the tor, so that you should now find yourself at Foxtor House in Foxtor Gert.

10 Follow the gert uphill right until the tip of a post is visible, indicating the entrance to -

C Black Lane (South). Follow the path, remaining on the left side beyond the post and always near the valley floor. The drained tarn where Wollake rises - it is the highest placed tributary of the River Erme -lies in the peat above the further (right) bank. Wet though it often is, the pass gives a sense of security and satisfaction at penetrating this wild country.

11 When the peat banks on either side close in, cross the stream and remain on the right bank. Notice the tor-less nature of the fen around you - only distant high points such as Three Burrows and Sharp Tor are visible.

12 Three quarters of a mile (1.2 km) through the pass will bring you to a point opposite a second post, leave it and branch right diagonally over the

hill. You will soon see a continuous line of tinners' stone mounds; they mark the edge of the valley of Duckspool Stream. Make for the nearest mound.

13 Cross the stream; the source mire expands above this point, and is dangerous. Follow the path (right) along the opposite bank to a conspicuous boulder.

D Duckspool. The pool, now a treacherous mire, was once a moorland tarn noted for its wildfowl (all species being known to the moormen as 'ducks'!), but was long ago drained by tinners. The boulder bears a bronze plaque commemorating the life's work of William Crossing (1848-1928), author of the classic Guide to Dartmoor (1909). In the cavity below is a copper canister - its lid also bearing a commemoration, this time to R C Carpenter, inaugurator of the post-box here in 1938. The canister contains a visitors' book, rubber stamp and ink pad.

Write your message, frank and deposit it for the next explorer to carry away; then 'clear the box' of previous mail. On the return walk take care to turn left from Foxtor Gert at Foxtor House (Note B), keeping Foxtor Head well to your right.

BIRCH TOR, CHALLACOMBE, VITIFER MINE

2½ miles (4 km) Moderately easy; dry. DANGER: flooded water-wheel pits

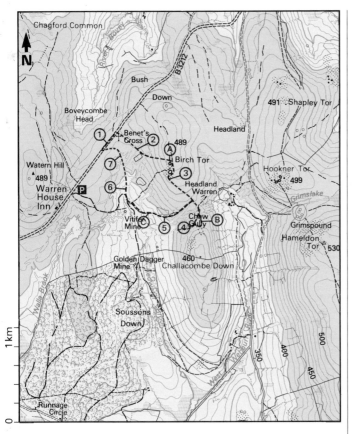

left and pass the corner of an enclosure; cross two gerts (the banks are very steep); beyond the second, follow a narrow branch path, left, to the tor above.

A Birch Tor has several piles. Go first to the highest placed (north) pile and see the view of north-east Dartmoor. From the southern main pile, look down into the valley of Redwater Brook containing the ruined buildings of the Birch Tor & Vitifer Mine and, further downstream, those of the Golden Dagger; Challacombe Down rises directly ahead.

2 *Walk towards the left side of Challacombe Down. Cross the Vitifer-Headland miners' path and notice the buildings of the former Headland Warren, left. Cross the heads of two gerts to a group of standing stones.*

B Challacombe Down triple stone row is a compact monument with a blocking stone at the higher end and the site of a grave at the lower. The kistvaen has disappeared, but the retaining circle remains. Signs exist in mid-row of a second grave.

4 *Return to the miners' path.*

5 *Descend left to the Redwater valley.*

C From the brink of Chaw Gully (left) peer into this 50 ft (15 m) deep gash in the dynamite-torn hillside.

6 *On reaching the ruined mine buildings follow the path beside Redwater Brook.* CAUTION: *it skirts the edge of a dangerous wheel pit.*

7 *When the path crosses the head of a gert, Benet's Cross and the car park come into sight. Return direct to the start.*

The Birch Tor & Vitifer Tine Mine continued to work, albeit in diminishing spasms, until the early 1930s, having provided employment for several generations of miners from Dartmoor hamlets and border-country villages. The scenery of the district is very striking, comprising rugged tors, mining gerts blasted by gunpowder and later dynamite and the sweeping backcloth of the Hameldon ridge. Take the B3212 road east from Two Bridges, or west from Moretonhampstead; half a mile (0.8 km) east of the Warren House Inn is a car park on the south side of the road: park there.

1 *Walk 150 yds (137 m) along the road to Benet's Cross, weather-beaten boundary mark (right). The incised letters 'WB' indicate 'Warren Bounds', (ie Headland Warren).*

2 *Follow a descending green path joining with one from the car park. Turn*

Walk 12

DR BLACKALL'S DRIVE AND MIL TOR

2½ miles (4 km) Easy; stony track; water lies after heavy rain

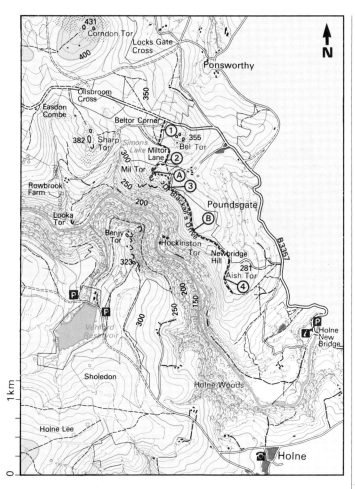

into the car park at Beltor Corner on Sherberton Common, two miles (3.2 km) east of Dartmeet.

1 *Follow the track beside the wall, left. As it zigzags towards Mil Tor - through Miltor Lane, Bel Tor is seen within enclosures, left.*

2 *At the end of Miltor Lane climb to Mil Tor, right.*

A Mil and Sharp Tors, occupying commanding positions above the gorge, are the most impressive of those so placed. Mil offers a splendid view as well as the sound of the river, completely covering the floor of its V-shaped valley 600 ft (183 m) below. There are four rock basins on the tor. Benjy Tor is directly opposite; although lower than Mil, it is impressive as the culmination of the almost sheer south valley-side.

3 *Return to Dr Blackall's Drive at Stumley Corner, the final right-angle bend in the zigzag series. From here the track runs south-west along the 1000 ft (304 m) contour and affords a constant view of the river below - often, with herons fishing at the rapids between islands.*

B Hockinston Tor, a pile in almost complete decay, lies on the slope below the track. Here the granite of the high moor gives place to border-country slates which, on the opposite side of the gorge are cleft by steep, trough-like tributary streams. Below the tor is the flood-plain of Hockingston Marsh.

4 *Aish Tor, high Dartmoor's final tor overlooking Dart, is so small as to be scarcely noticeable. After passing its foot turn back before losing height on Newbridge hill and return to the start.*

A prestigious undertaking among 19th century gentry was the making of scenic carriage drives. Thus in the 1870s Dr Joseph Blackall of Spitchwick Manor, made this scenically exciting road along the brink of the Double Dart Gorge: it is consequently known as 'Dr Blackall's Drive'. NOTE: As no satisfactory alternative return walking route is available this is an out-and-return single-route walk. Take the B3357 road west from Ashburton or east from Two Bridges. Turn

RYDERS RINGS AND BLACK TOR (AVON)

3½ miles (5.6 km) Do not attempt in mist; highland peaty and wet; gradients moderately easy.

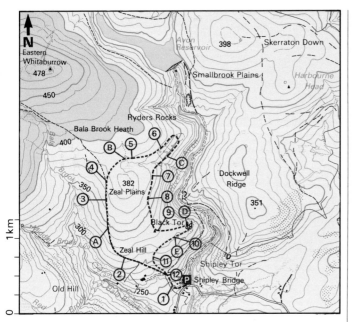

Avon - its ancient name was 'Aune' and the huge mire at its source is still known as Aune Head - is the longest of the southern Dartmoor rivers (22 miles/35 km). Its former glories in Shipley Gorge are somewhat diminished by the extraction of water upstream for the South West Water Authority's impounding reservoir, but it is still a beautiful sight, its long, glistening thread in Long-a-Traw and its rush over stepped, granite bedding in the shallow gorge delighting countless visitors. This walk provides views over the tributary valley of Bala Brook, before taking in the large prehistoric settlement of Ryders Rings, and Black Tor poised above the main valley. Drive from South Brent to Shipley Bridge and park in the car park on the west bank of the river, site of the former Brent Moor China Clay works.

1 *Follow the steep track which leaves the road beside a wall (left) and ascends behind the old works. Cross the road leading to the waterworks filtration plant (left) and continue the ascent beside the next wall (left).*

2 *The track remains clear beyond the highest wall corner. It is actually the trackbed of a tramroad laid down in 1846 to bring peat to an earlier works. Notice granite sets (blocks) with remaining iron spikes which once held wooden rails in place. The gradient eases on the shoulder of Zeal Hill.*

A Viewpoint: from rocks beside the track: moorward, right to left, Eastern Whitaburrow, Bala Brook valley, Knattaburrow, Middle Brook, Old Hill, the huge Three Burrows, Wacka Tor, Brent Fore Hill, Henchertraw (Red Brook valley), Hickley Ridge and Ugborough Beacon Rocks rising behind; in-country, South Hams, Erme, Avon and Dart estuaries, English Channel.

3 *Continue until the track is comparatively level and curves to the left ahead. It continues across Bala Brook Heath below Eastern Whitaburrow.*

4 *Just before the curve, a series of boulders beside the track (left) ends with a pointed stone. Here leave the track and make across the moor, right, towards a dark (heather-covered) hillside. The moor, here known as Zeal Plains, is featureless; to ensure correct direction watch for the highest edge of border-country enclosures in the mid-distance; a mire will appear close by on your right.*

B Dry Brook Gully channels the stream rising in the mire. Tinworks abound and Avon's east valley-side is now seen in detail.

5 *Keep well to the left of the mire, cross tinners' gerts and descend the hill parallel to the gully.*

6 *An old leat channel is seen (right) crossing the gully, and the wall of a pound will soon appear, left. Make for this, crossing the same leat channel near the pound.*

C Ryders Rings is an enclosed village of the early Bronze Age divided into two areas by a partitioning wall; containing 34 huts and numerous sheep pens built against

Over

the perimeter wall, the pound has three entrances. It is a larger village than the celebrated Grimspound (See Walk 21), with a more remote setting. There are fine views, again over the South Hams to the English Channel, seen between Shipley Tor and Black Tor, and the river can be heard passing through Shipley Gorge.

7 *Walk south below the leat; cross Dry Brook Gully (here well below the head-mire) and regain the leat, which will guide you above the large bracken field ahead.*

8 *Black Tor appears on the hill-spur, left - but, for a short way, maintain your present height just below the leat, which is seen above, right.*

9 *Make half-left for a mound on the plain below - a ruined cairn. Walk straight from it to the tor.*

D Black Tor occupies a Rhine-castle position on the spur overlooking Long-a-Traw, the trough-like reach of Avon below the reservoir. There are several rockpiles. It is striking to view, from the main pile, the north pile outlined against the flank of Woolholes Plain beyond the river, and the huge sweep of Zeal Plains, left.

10 *Walk towards lower Red Brook valley for 200 yds (183 m), to groups of stones seen on the upper fringe of a bracken field.*

E The stones are those of a Bronze Age farmhouse (hut circle) and pound, set within its own field system. The view from here includes South Brent town in the Avon valley at the foot of the border-country.

11 *Continue direction of walk (around fringe of bracken) until the Water Works filtration plant is visible.*

12 *Descend to the Water Works road; cross, follow path beside wall to the start.*

Walk 14
SHARP TOR AND DOUBLE DART GORGE
4 miles (6.4 km) Steep, slippery and wet; 400 ft (122 m) climb at end

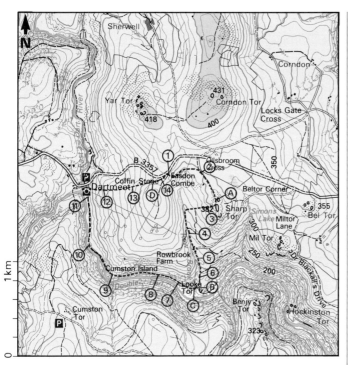

2 *Cross the infant Row Brook (Row rhymes with cow), pass an isolated rockpile and make for the central gap in the rock.*

A Sharp Tor (Double Dart) Although ravaged by Ice Age weathering it is easy to visualise Sharp Tor's original conical shape. Do not ascend the rockpile in a high wind. Outstanding in the view are the wooded, interlocking spurs of the gorge, the glinting reaches of the river, and Benjy Tor across the valley. The roofs of Rowbrook Farm below, right, mark the next objective.

3 *To avoid clitter, gorse and bracken, follow a path leading to trees at the head of the combe.*

4 *When near Row Brook, turn left and follow the left bank to the gate of Rowbrook Farm, where the sound of the river in the gorge is audible. Enter the farmyard, go to the back door of the farmhouse (right), knock loudly and show your copy of WALK DARTMOOR before requesting permission to cross the farmland.*

5 *From the farmyard enter a gate immediately right, marked 'Private -No right of way'. Follow the lane alongside an old building; cross the field beyond and pass through the next gateway.*

6 *Descend to a narrow, transverse path; follow it (right) to a tree-shrouded crag, left, at hillside level.*

B Looka Tor. This extraordinary pile, appearing on approach merely to be a rock-ledge, actually rises from the very river bank below - an interesting example of a valley-floor

Over

The great V-shaped cleft through which the united East and West Dart rivers - thus 'Double Dart' - leave their birthland is in places 600 ft (183 m) deep. If there has been heavy rain and the river is 'up', the walk will be all the more spectacular. On the brink of the gorge sides are fine tors, their clitters streaming down the wooded hillsides to the river bank and harbouring many varieties of trees, including strangely misshapen oaks. The tors lining the east/north brink are Sharp, Mil and Hockinston opposite are Benjy and Cumston Tors. This walk is not suitable for young children, nor for an adult carrying a child in a back-sling. Boots with non-slip cleats are essential. Also note that pre-permission to pass through the fields of Rowbrook Farm must be obtained from the tenant, Mrs May. If possible call before 1100 hrs; no polite request is ever refused, but dogs are not allowed. Park in the spacious car park on the south roadside (B3357) at the top of Dartmeet Hill.

1 *Follow the descending path towards Sharp Tor. Do not continue to the valley bottom (Easdon Combe) but turn left into a transverse path rounding the head of the combe.*

30

tor. The view from the crag towards Mil Tor and the river is striking. Its old name, Eagle Rock, recalls traditions of the Dartmoor golden eagle, reputed to have had an eyrie on this crag. Its more modern name is a corruption of Lookout Tor, for here the smugglers kept watch for excisemen while their companions hid contraband below.

C Double Dart Gorge. Return to the main path and descend to it. Walk left and approach near to Looka Tor.

7 *Walk up the main valley, cross Row Brook and follow a path under the rocky hillside (right) which gradually links with the river bank, where you may be surprised by the swift and dangerous current below.*

8 *The path becomes difficult, necessitating an inescapable scramble above former lengths of path eroded by the river; the immense platform of granite bedding in the river below is known as 'Broada Stones'.*

9 *When the path becomes easier, notice a rectangular stone pit beside it and funnel walls reaching from the pit to the rock masses, right. This unique object is a warrener's vermin-drowning trap.*

10 *Pass Cumston Island, noticing Cumston Tor high above the further bank. At length the few houses of Dartmeet hamlet are glimpsed through the trees. Follow the path round the higher side of a small enclosure; the meeting of the Dart rivers is opposite this point.*

11 *Reaching the further, north end of the enclosure, do not pass through the gateway in the fence, but take the green path, right. It soon becomes a steep ascent of Vag Hill, from which you will see below left the Dartmeet car park, the approaching East Dart River and traffic on the B3357.*

12 *The road bears away from the path, which pursues a direct course to the north (left) shoulder of Vag Hill.*

13 *When the road is furthest from the path, notice that a sunken track has come in sight (below, left) between the two - but nearer the path. This is the ancient way to Ashburton and Widecombe-in-the-Moor from the central basin via Dartmeet clapper bridge. A large, flat boulder can now be seen beside the old track; make for this.*

D This is the 'Coffin Stone'. Here, in days when bearers had to carry the dead of the Ancient Tenements to Widecombe church for burial, they set down their burden and rested. A number of crosses and initials appear on the face of the stone, carved by bearers who were not anxious to resume their toil on this long, punishing slope!

14 *On reaching the crest of the hill, the car park at the start of the walk will at once come in sight.*

Walk 15

VIXEN, HECKWOOD AND PU TORS

3¾ miles (6 km) Very easy; dry

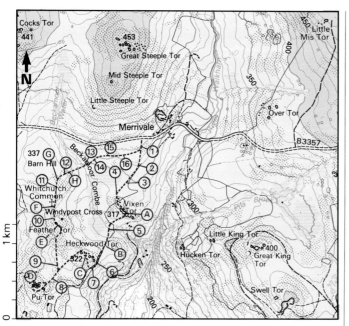

3 *At the wall corner, walk ahead to a rock-group outside the wall of Vixen Tor Newtake. A notice-board requests the use of 'the stile provided' to approach the tor. On your way, notice an inscribed Whitchurch-Sampford bond-stone.*

4 *Cross the stile and proceed to Vixen Tor.*

A Vixen Tor. This immense, grotesque pile stands 93 ft (28 m) above the ground on the lower side, and 52 ft (16 m) on the higher. Rock basins on the summit are seen only by those bold enough to attain it and a shallow cave exists on the south side. Legend claims that the witch of Vixen Tor lured travellers into Vixentor Mire. It is obvious that every other visible tor is higher than Vixen.

5 *Continue to next stile; cross Beckamoor Water at a ford beside the wall (left). Ascend the hill ahead, passing another bond-stone.*

B Viewpoint (scenery typically Dartmoor): the valley of Beckamoor Water points towards Cocks Tor; right of it are the tors of Little, Mid and Great Steeple, Great and Little Mis, and the low-lying Over Tor beyond Long Ash Newtake.

6 *Follow a cart track to Heckwood Quarry; notice large, dressed granite block; this was shaped for the new Plymouth Breakwater of 1812, but abandoned due to flaw.*

7 *Turn right from the track to -*

C Heckwood Tor, originally a very large pile; severe weathering has resulted in a widespread rockfield on the summit plateau. Notice extensive deciduous woodlands in the

West Dartmoor's River Walkham flows below some of the Moor's finest tors. A ridge running due south from Whit Tor (on Langstone Moor) declines to its foot above Sampford Spiney village with a final flourish at Pu Tor. Great Mis Tor is lord of the range, while Vixen Tor's lowly elevation is balanced by a remarkable and distinctive character. Facing Great Mis Tor across the valley are Roos and Great Steeple Tors. But this walk lies on the south spur of the ridge. Take the B3357 road east from Tavistock ascending the Moor's escarpment at Pork Hill. After crossing a plain, the road descends to the Walkham valley at Merrivale; as the descent begins

watch for a small, sunken car park, which you will see on the left as you continue on the road from Tavistock. Walk along the road from the car park to the starting point.

NOTE: Dogs are not allowed in Vixen Tor Newtake, which it is necessary to enter to reach the tor.

1 *Cross the road and follow the corn-ditch wall, left, towards Vixen Tor (likened at this angle to an 'old man in cap with back to wife'). Further ahead are Heckwood and Pu Tors; across the valley (left) are hut circles and antiquities on Long Ash Plain.*

2 *Cross the Grimstone leat on a cart bridge. Notice, right of Pu Tor, the piles of Feather Tor, the diminutive Barn Hill Rocks, and the Windypost Cross in the intervening dip.*

Over

lower Walkhem valley.

8 *Follow the path, cross a leat and ascend direct to -*

D Pu Tor. This, a landmark from afar (despite its modest 1025 ft (312 m),) contains a natural grass 'court', an inner recess, overlooked by the four piles of the tor in the manner of guard-towers. Rock basins are numerous. Quarrying and surface-granite working on this common has left many interesting granite shapes.

9 *Walk towards the Cocks-Great Steeple ridge. Cross the leat again and make for a low-lying rockpile in a dip ahead. Cross the winding leat twice more to reach -*

E Feather Tor. Although not a high rockpile, its primeval dimensions may be judged from the immense clitter surrounding it; views westward into Cornwall are very fine.

10 *Walk towards Cocks Tor (left of Great Steeple Tor) and make for a*

granite cross.

F Windypost Cross. The seven foot (2.1 m) stance of this aptly named monument on a windswept ridge marks the passage across the hill of the ancient Jobbers' Road. Observe here the interesting traditional Dartmoor method of controlling the water supply of a branch-leat by a perforated stone; this is called a 'bull's eye'

11 *Make for the lower of two small rock-groups ahead -*

G Barn Hill Rocks, which allows a fine view of the torscape. Brent Tor brings the eye back to the western escarpment of the Moor.

12 *Next follow a direct line towards the block-like Little Mis Tor. Descend, cross a disused leat and make for the ruined -*

H 'Blacksmith's Shop' which once served the local quarries. A fine wheelwright's stone lies outside the ruin, the Grimstone leat flows past it, and a fording place is visible on

the stream below.

13 *Descend to Beckamoor Ford. On the stream's right bank is a large, pointed boulder and below it, a tinners' house which has lost one end to stream erosion. The ford has picturesque, sunken approaches and remnant stepping stones. On the left bank are two Sampford Spiney bondstones.*

14 *Leave the track above the east bank and walk to the Grimstone leat, here approaching Beckamoor Combe.*

15 *Cross a wide card bridge over the leat and walk upstream. When passing the foot of the lowest clitter deposit under Little Steeple Tor, notice that Vixen Tor, now the Egyptian Sphinx, returns, as you walk, to its first image as man-in-cap-and-wife.*

16 *Leave the leat and walk toward Over Tor (left of highway beyond valley). The starting point will soon appear.*

Walk 16

CUMSTON TOR AND HOLNE RIDGE

3 miles (4.8 km) Some wet, peaty ground; trackless open moor; 400 ft (122 m) climb

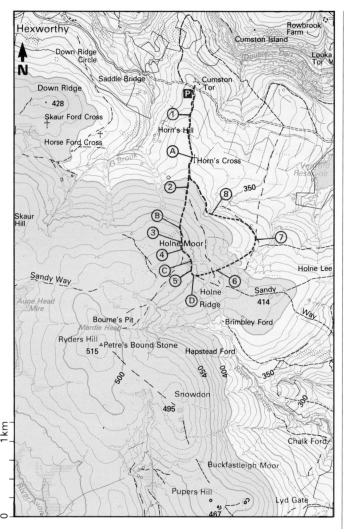

mit rock. Turn your back on the river below and look south to the crest of Holne Ridge, a rise in the land of 800 ft (244 m). Holne Ridge is the eastern portion of the southern Dartmoor hill-chain so often mentioned in this Guide. It also is the watershed between Dart country (*ie,* the central basin) and the rivers rising on the southern moor - Plym, Yealm, Erme, Avon and Harbourne. Panoramic views for Holne Ridge will amply reward the walker for the easy climb involved.

Branch south from the B3357 road two thirds of a mile (1 km) west of Dartmeet, and pass through Huccaby and Hexworthy. Following the zigzag ascent above the Forest Inn, continue to Saddle Bridge (0 Brook); ascend to Cumston Tor and turn into the hilltop car park, left. Either on arrival or departure, visit the tor.

1 *Cross the road and follow the broad, green path up Horn's Hill to a flat plain. Notice the nearby field system. Continue to a granite cross now in view.*

A Horn's Cross, an ancient relic of the trans-Dartmoor monastic way series where the monastic path is well defined on either side.

2 *Take the ascent ahead. Pass a bondstone (marked 'PUDC' - Paignton Urban District Council), left, on the boundary of the Venford reservoir catchment area and a large cairn, right. Cross a disused leat and reach another bond-stone.*

B Viewpoint: Bellever Tor rises from the floor of the central basin, overlooked in the north by the basin

Over

This walk should not be attempted if mist or high wind seems likely. Cumston Tor occupies a sentinel position on the south brink of the Double Dart Gorge, and affords good views of Dartmeet and of the tors on the far side of the gorge culminating in Yar and Corndon Tors. Several rock basins occur, the largest on the easily attainable sum-

rim. Beyond the reservoir are Dartmoor's eastern highlands, while nearer, Down Ridge declines to the 0 Brook valley.

3 *Continue the ascent, disregarding a well-defined track branching left. Cross a reave. Hills seen in the east beyond Dartmoor are the Haldon Hills (beyond which lies the Exe valley). Watch for a large, pointed boulder, left, about 100 yds (91 m) away: another, nearer bond-stone stands to the right. Ahead is a 'false crest'; higher and further (right) is the ridge of Skaur Hill.*

4 *After passing between pointed boulder and bond-stone, bear away left to a low mound on the skyline - the base of a destroyed cairn. The ground now becomes peaty and wet. Go to a nearby series of mining mounds.*

C The estuary of the River Teign and the vale of Dart; the rise to the Moor from the border country at Wallaford Down, and the successive upwards steps of Pupers, Snowdon and Ryder, make this a fine viewpoint.

5 *Walk towards the Snowdon-Ryder col to reach another bond-stone.*

D Viewpoint: sweeping decline of this great ridge to Holne Lee and its northern off-shoot, Sholedon. The valley nearest ahead channels a branch of Venford Brook in Ringleshutes Gert. Buckfastleigh town lies in the Mardle valley; left of it, beyond the top of Holne Lee (and beneath a prominent hilltop copse) is the tower of Buckfast Abbey.

6 *Follow the direction of the line of PUDC bond-stones until you see the reservoir, left; then bear left and head towards Yar Tor. This will entail crossing two deep gerts, but animal paths across them can always be found. Both are workings of the former Ringleshutes Tin Mine.*

7 *Below the second gert is a good path pointing slightly left of Yar Tor; follow this and the distant Cumston Tor and car park will (momentarily) come into sight, until both are lost behind the outline of Horn's Hill.*

8 *In descending, notice the north side of the Double Dart Gorge (right). The broad green way beyond Horn's Cross appears below. Return to the start.*

Walk 17
SWINCOMBE
2 miles (3.2 km) Very easy

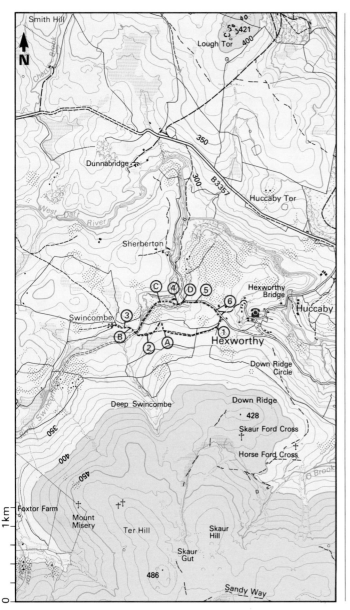

This is a pastoral walk amid gentle hills that know no tors, no rugged clitters, no rock-ridges nor precipitious slopes. The silver thread of the little River Swincombe provides the theme of this picture of a sequestered corner of Dartmoor's central basin. The name 'Swincombe' also attaches to the tiny settlement in its middle reach valley, at a point where an historic track crosses the river. Branch south from the B3357 road, two thirds of a mile (1 km) west of Dartmeet, and pass through Huccaby and Hexworthy. At the head of the zig-zag hill past the Forest Inn, turn hairpin right and drive for a third of a mile (0.5 km) to a wide opening (left) between newtake walls, where a stony track approaches the road. Park here, but not on the track.

1 *Follow the track, which bears right and passes through a gateway below the old Wheal Emma leat channel. Down Ridge is above, left, and a pleasant view of the Swincombe valley opens before you. When the track begins to descend towards the river, leave it and walk, right, to the ruins of a cottage.*

A Dolly Trebble's House. Here in widowhood lived a lady whose captivating charms in her early years were said to have attracted the attentions of the Prince Regent, later George IV, when on a visit to Dartmoor. The little house, built in the late 18th century, still has its fireplace jambs and attached garden and paddock enclosures.

2 *Rejoin the track and descend to the river.*

Over

B Swincombe The three traditional methods of crossing a river are here side by side - bridge, stepping stones, ford. The wooden bridge is 'Fairy Bridge' (pixie undertones!) and the ford is the crossing place of the ancient packhorse track between Ashburton and Tavistock which you have followed from Hexworthy. On the west bank is an interesting ruin, properly named Lower Swincombe but known always as 'John Bishop's House', which was·built and occupied by a locally celebrated granite mason of that name, one and a half centuries ago. Notice the porch roofed by granite 'steps', Further upstream is the ruin of Higher Swincombe; the house nearby is of the early 20th century. The track here passes between pretentious (but crumbling) gateposts; these were built by Sir Thomas Tyrwhitt (1762-1833) - Black Rod in the House of Commons and close friend of the Prince Regent - who acquired the Swincombe settlement as an addition to his Tor Royal estate near Princetown.

3 *Return to the river. Cross. Follow the hard road, left, which is for vehicular access to the little reservoir upstream. The river has picturesque bends and falls in this reach. When the road reaches a right-hand bend on a high bank above the river, leave it and descend to the plain below.*

C Gobbet Plain has interesting tinworking remains. First, directly under the bank is seen the ruin of a blowing house; this possesses a rare feature in the shape of both upper and lower grindstones of a clazing (ore-grinding) mill, by which means the tin-ore was crushed before the invention of water wheel-powered drop-stamps. This means that the house is not later than early 15th century in origin. Mortar stones within the ruin, point to its continued use well into the 17th century. There are also two mould-stones. The leat from the river and the water-wheel pit are traceable.

4 *Follow the road for 200 yds (183 m).*

D A large oblong pit below the road contained the water wheel of the 19th century Gobbet Tin Mine;

the leat is seen on the high bank above the road, over which it was aqueducted through a wooden launder (a channel on trestles). Ruins of mine buildings on the plain include a 'counting house' (office), some of its masonry consisting of stones removed from the ancient blowing house nearby. The mine failed, and equipment was sold to pay overdue land rent, in 1876. Across the river arc scen the buildings of Sherberton Farm, an Ancient Tenement, and in the enclosures are several beehives, the property of Buckfast Abbey, for the production of heather honey.

5 *Pass through the gateway ahead; turn right into the Sherberton-Hexworthy road. Notice the granite portal of a tunnel, right, an adit of Gobbet Mine later adapted by Paignton Water Works to carry the water-pipe from their Swincombe reservoir through the hill to the impounding reservoir at Venford.*

6 *To reach the starting point, follow the road.*

CATOR COMMON AND PIZWELL ANCIENT TENEMENT
2 miles (3.2 km) Very easy; dry

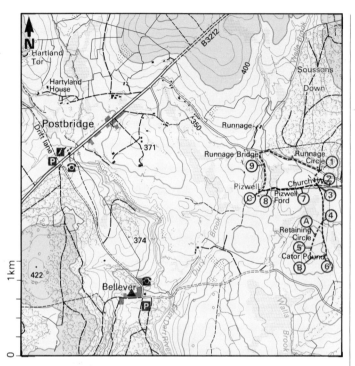

is Church Way - and enters a gate beside a 'Bridle path' fingerpost.

4 *Follow the track; it passes an extensive mire, right, then veers to the left side of a rounded hill ahead. Leave the track and walk (right) to a mound on the hill-crest.*

A The mound is the base of a cairn that once was raised over an interment; the central hollow formerly contained the kistvaen. Removal of the cairn has revealed a fine retaining circle of some 25 remaining stones. The lack of height here does not diminish the pleasing and clearly defined view over the central basin.

5 *Walk towards a nearby small plantation (right); cross a transverse reave; on meeting a converging reave, join it and walk to the left until some set stones come into view. These form the wall of -*

B Cator Pound, a rectangular enclosure of great antiquity, which was approached by a droveway on the south-west side.

6 *Walk eastward to rejoin the track to the gate (Note 3).*

7 *Turn left into Church Way; cross Walla Brook at Pizwell Ford.*

C Pizwell. Walk between the buildings, then return and re-cross Walla Brook. The lowest placed building of the tenement is a medieval longhouse which, now in use as a store, was occupied until 1935.

8 *Either - return along Church Way and cross the common towards the opening in the trees and the start.*

9 *Or - follow the pleasant right bank of Walla Brook upstream to Runnage Bridge, turning right at the road ro reach the start.*

Dartmoor's medieval history is uniquely represented by the splendid group of buildings at Pizwell in the central basin, the originals of a tenement cluster of three farms documented in 1260. Although nowadays, due to cost, tin or slate has replaced thatch, all the buildings are almost as they were. Even the ford and the stepping stones over Walla Brook (a tributary of East Dart) and the stony road approaching the ford between heather banks remains unaffected by modern trends. The road is the ancient Church Way between Pizwell and Widecombe-in-the-Moor.

Branch right from the B3212 one mile (1.6 km) east of Postbridge Post Office, at the sign 'Widecombe'. Cross Walla Brook at Runnage Bridge and continue half a mile (0.8 km) ahead to an opening in the Soussons plantations, left. Park on the wide grass verge.

1 *In the opening is an almost perfect Bronze Age retaining circle, with two side-stones of the central kistvaen still in place.*

2 *Cross the common opposite towards the cone of Bellever Tor (seen above the Bellever plantations). At a wide transverse track, turn left.*

3 *The track intersects a stony road - this*

BENJY TOR

2½ miles (4 km) Very easy; dry

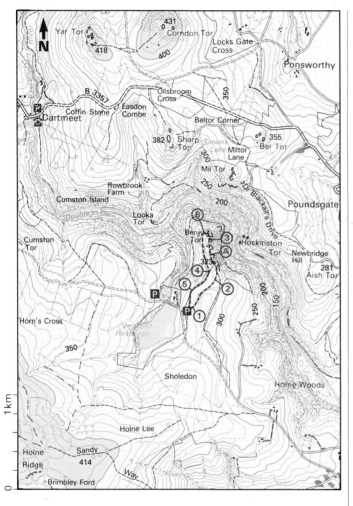

2 *On reaching a banked-up leat, follow it (left) and continue parallel to the nearby Stoke corn-ditch wall, right. The rock-crowned mound of Benjy Tor will appear ahead; walk near the wall in approaching the tor in order to avoid a large bracken field, left.*

A Benjy Tor consists of several piles on a rock-ridge 500 yds (457 m) in length, and provides striking views into the Double Dart Gorge; the scenic Dr Blackall's Drive appears on the opposite brink zigzagging under rugged Mil Tor and passing above Hockinston Tor. Sharp Tor rises to break the outlines of Yar and Corndon Tors. From the larger of the two north piles, its rockface falling precipitously to the river, one sees in detail Mil Tor and the valley of Simon's Lake as well as the straight trough of Row Brook and the roofs of Rowbrook Farm further up the valley.

3 *Walk to the smaller north pile; double back, left, and follow a clear path below the west side of the rock-ridge.*

B The tributary valley of Venford Brook is below, right. Beyond it, notice the marks of long-disused medieval enclosures on the moor, backed by the lofty Holne Ridge.

4 *The path passes through bracken and joins a broad, grass path coming down from the south pile. Turn right into this.*

5 *Take the left fork to the car park (a right fork would take you to the reservoir). Water seen foaming into the reservoir on the further bank is piped from the small Swincombe reservoir. (See Walk 17, Note 5).*

Many of Dartmoor's most attractive features lie hidden from the casual eye. In approaching Benjy Tor from the west there is no hint of the breath-taking spectacle to come. It is an exciting tor for children, easily climbable and with crevices and caverns which can be seen on the summit plateau not too near the brink of the gorge. Take the Holne-Hexworthy road to the east side of Venford reservoir; car park, left.

1 *Follow a green path uphill from the back of the car park.*

39

BROADUN, SANDY HOLE, WATERFALLS

5½ miles (8.8 km) Some very uneven ground; climb 600 ft (183 m); mostly dry

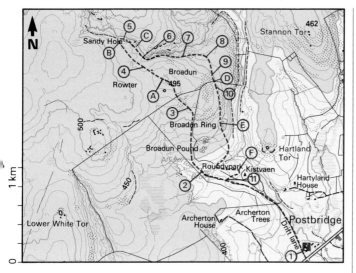

The River Dart, from which the Moor took its name in Saxon times, has the longest moorland course (11.6 miles/18.6 km) of the 15 main rivers pouring from its high peatlands. The river rises in the northern fen as two branches, which unite at Dartmeet. West Dart is slightly longer than its sister stream, East Dart, which has the higher source at 1840 ft (561 m) above sea level. Both rivers flow through the central basin, where they receive many tributaries before their united plunge into the Double Dart Gorge. This walk leads to the section of the East Dart river between its upper and middle reaches. Take the B3212 road to Postbridge and park in the official car park near the Post Office.

1 *Mount the stile at the higher end of the car park and turn right into a wide, grassy way known as 'Drift Lane'; East Dart flows near you,*
right. Pass through Drift Lane Gate at Archerton Trees, beyond which the track continues as a stony road.

2 *Two fords (on branches of Archerton Brook) take the track to a massive clapper cart bridge over the old Powder Mills leat, then towards a wall corner, from where it ascends Broadun beside the wall (right).*

3 *Stay on the track until near the hillcrest. Notice another wall ascending the hill 200 yds (183 m) to your left, surmounted by two humps; walk across to the lower left hand hump. Mount a stile near the wall corner and continue to climb the hill.*

A On the summit of Broadun, there is a striking view of the wild north moor, including Cut Hill (just below 2000 ft (610 m). In the East Dart valley is seen the mouth of a small gorge known as 'Sandy Hole' and below it the cataract known simply as 'Waterfalls'.

4 *Descend the hill towards Sandy Hole by-passing the cataract.*

B At Sandy Hole, near the end of the river's long upper reach the river bed was excavated by medieval tinners to induce a swift current to carry away waste from their workings. The river has deposited huge quantities of sandy gravel (hence Sandy Hole) near a pool suitable for safe family swimming, but not diving; there are submerged rocks.

5 *Follow the right bank downstream to Waterfalls.*

C At Waterfalls, the river spouts diagonally across the edge of fine-grained granite to begin its descent to the central basin. Mosses and lichens adorn the rocks, and heather and gorse sprout from cavities in the granite. Following an acute bend downstream, the river plunges into another small gorge - Broadun Hole.

6 *From Waterfalls take the well-defined path along the hillside. The serpentine hole, set amid big hills is very picturesque.*

7 *Ignore an uphill path branching right.*

8 *As the river loops eastward, follow the path straight ahead, where it makes a short cut high above a grassy plain.*

9 *Below the corner of a fenced wall right, pause and study the view.*

D Viewpoint. Beyond the trees and fields of the central basin is a view extending left to right, from Buckland Beacon to the East Dart valley below Broadun Hole.

10 *The path above the river passes through two broken walls ahead.*

E The river appears ahead as it

Over

40

approaches Postbridge. On the near side of Archerton Trees above the river, and beside a circular enclosure, is 'Roundypark' kistvaen. Make for this by-passing some hut circles, descending to the valley of Archerton Brook and mounting the opposite valley side.

F Roundypark kistvaen is a massive example of a prehistoric sepulchre, doubtless associated with the hut circle village above.

11 *From a gate in the nearby fence rejoin the track to Postbridge.*

GRIMSPOUND, HAMELDON TOR, KINGS BARROW
3 miles (4.8 km) Beginning strenuous (direct climb of 400 ft/122 m)

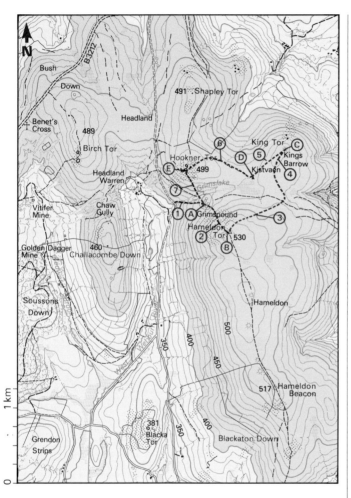

The celebrated early Bronze Age village of Grimspound receives thousands of visitors each year. It is easy to reach and its massive pound encloses the remains of 24 huts, several with protected entrance passages. The village water supply, Grims Lake, forms the central thread of this walk, and is overlooked by the fine Hookner Tor and the smaller, but much higher, Hameldon Tor. Kings Barrow, on a spur looking far out to east Devon, was probably the grave of a Grimspound chieftan with a discerning eye for a final resting place with a

view! The best travel approach is from the north; branch south at Challacombe Cross on the B3212 road (2 miles/3.2 km, east of the Warren House Inn, a famous hostelry); 1.4 miles (2.2 km) along this modern pass road, cut in 1874, will bring you (after topping the Headland col with its splendid view of southern Dartmoor) to a small roadside parking space;· the house (under its 'monkey-puzzle' trees) and enclosures of Headland Warren lie below, right. Three coaches (many do stop here) fill the space, so an early morning visit is recommended.

1 *Ascend steps in the roadside opposite the parking space; follow the path which, after only a short distance, crosses Grims Lake and reaches a huge pound.*

A Grimspound. There are many things to observe here. The pound has been built to enclose the rush-filled valley of Grims Lake, so that the people could draw their water without leaving the pound. The great south gateway, built of massive dry stone masonry and re-taining its original paving, was closed by huge timbers. A hut beside the path leading to the gateway, has a good entrance passage and the view beyond the nearby humpy outline of Challacombe Down extends to the Warren House Inn and Princetown.

2 *Pass through the great gateway and climb the steep path ahead to -*

B Hameldon Tor. This consists of several small, ruined rockpiles, the summit being marked by an Ord-

Over

nance Survey triangulation pillar. Points to note are: north - High Willes and Yes Tor on their 2000 ft (610 m) ridge and, to the right, the north-east escarpment of the Moor, and much of north Devon; north-east - Castle Drogo (the last castle to be built in England) above Fingle Gorge, and Exmoor beyond; east -the Haldon Hills and Haldon Belvedere (folly tower), the Exe valley and Somerset's Blackdown Hills; south-east - the Moor's escarpment punctuated by Black Hill, Hey Tor, Rippen Tor and intermediate rockpiles; south and south-west - the splendid ten mile (16 km) hill-chain of southern Dartmoor; west - across the central basin to its further rim; north-west - Cut Hill (250 ft/76 m higher than your present viewpoint) and the heights of the northern fen. The nearby north-easterly rise in the land is to Kings Barrow.

3 *Walk towards Kings Barrow. When a large tract of heather appears ahead, walk along its upper edge until you see a path penetrating its centre and leading to the shallow upper valley, left, of Grims Lake. Follow this path*

above the head-mire of the stream; it intersects the well-defined Natsworthy-Headland miners' path, beyond which, leave it and make for a standing stone on the hill-slope, right.

4 *This is one of a line of bond-stones bearing the letter 'B', marking the outer boundary between North Bovey and Manaton parishes. Continue from here towards the hill-crest where, after walking 30 yds (27 m), a large mound will be seen -*

C Kings Barrow. This ancient sepulchre is on the tip of an eastward promontory of the high moor. It is a large, but sadly ruined cairn where, no doubt, a chieftan was buried to the accompaniment of religious rites long lost to us. The view from this spur centres on the old border town of Moretonhampstead and extends to the estuary of the Dartmoor River Teign and its entry into the English Channel at Teignmouth. The small tor (King Tor) on the hillside below is not visible from the barrow.

5 *Hookner Tor now stands boldly in the west to the right of Hameldon Tor, but start by making for the*

lower Hameldon slope in order to avoid another heather patch - the plant is particularly luxuriant in summer on this high and dry easterly col. On meeting a broad path pointing towards Hookner (right), follow it for a short way, then make for a group of set stones left of the path.

D The stones are the remains of Hookner kistvaen and retaining circle; this grave had, unusually, two cover-stones; one is pushed aside but its companion remains in position.

6 *To avoid yet more, even deeper heather between the kistvaen and Hookner Tor, return to the broad path. Follow it, left, to the shoulder of the tor, then leave it and walk to the rocks.*

E Hookner Tor has several piles; it is highly effective to stand on the highest and study the lower and larger piles outlined against the West Webburn valley and the southern hill-chain.

7 *Descend by a stony path below the main pile to Grimspound. Cross Grims Lake and turn right into the path descending to the start.*

Walk 22

GREAT HOUND AND GREA TORS

2½ miles (4 km) Very easy; dry

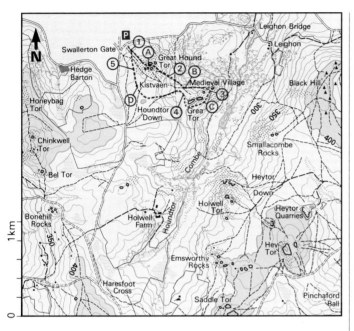

'Houndtor' should properly be 'Great Hound Tor', for there is a 'Little Hound Tor' on the north moor. It is the centre of an area of superstition and legend - even its name may have sprung from the legendary, spectral black hound of Dartmoor encountered on the tor as recently as 1965. Like Hey Tor, it is easily reached and there is a car park at Swallerton Gate (near the former 'Houndtor Inn'). Great Hound Tor is the gateway to an area rich in natural, unspoilt beauty, with Grea Tor and Houndtor Combe forming its centre-piece. Take the Chagford-Ashburton road to Swallerton Gate, one and a half miles (2.4 km) south of Heatree Cross and turn into the car park.

1 *Follow the broad path to the tor.*
A Great Hound Tor, a natural granite citadel, is a double 'avenue' tor, where Ice Age weathering has removed decayed rock to form parallel avenues between remaining rockpiles, of which the northern is most impressive. Walk through this, observing the cavities, pillars, shelves and gargantuan blocks on either side. At the far end of the avenue the heights above Houndtor Combe appear beyond Grea Tor; below, in a dip near Grea Tor, are the outlines of ruined buildings.
2 *Follow the path to the buildings, the remains of -*
B Houndtor Down medieval village. Excavation has revealed a settlement of 11 buildings, probably

pre-Conquest in origin when houses were of wattle and turf. Some are longhouses, some auxiliary buildings; several houses show traces of fireplaces, and one has an entrance passage with a cooler (a chamber built into the wall facing north-east to avoid sunlight). Like so many longhouses on the Moor, these are likely to have been emptied by the scourge of the Black Death in 1348. The situation of this village is not merely beautiful, but dramatic.
3 *Walk from the village to the lowest pile (left) of -*
C Grea Tor. There are in all five piles, increasing proportionately in size and elevation. Notice the contrasting sheet-like masses of aplite in the largest pile and the prevailing, coarse-grained granite of the others. The view across Houndtor Combe is of Holwell Tor rising to fine effect.
4 *Return towards Great Hound Tor; turn left into a clear, transverse track to the crest of Houndtor Down. Fork right to pass north (right) of a small tarn (sometimes dry); walk north-west to standing stones ahead.*
D Houndtor Down kistvaen. Had not the road-makers a century ago, rifled the kisvaen for stones, which they are known to have done, this would be a striking monument; now, the west segment of the retaining kerb-cicle (one with the stones close-set), the cover-stone and one side-stone have disappeared. The two prominent tors seen west of the road are, left to right, Chinkwell and Honeybag.
5 *Return over the moor to the now visible car park.*

BONEHILL ROCKS TO HONEYBAG TOR

2½ miles (4 km) Moderately easy; dry

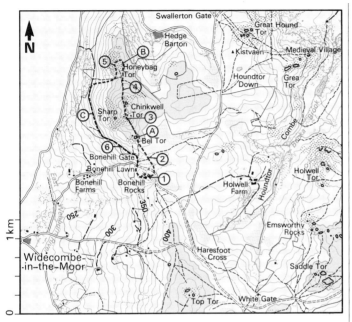

The crinkled top of Honeybag Tor and the smoother mound of Chinkwell comprise the northern end of a range of 12 tors extending south to Auswell Rocks. Those selected here afford fine views over the vale of Widecombe-in-the-Moor, with the village, celebrated both for its fair and 'cathedral of the Moor' church tower, nestling in mid-vale. The rugged tors east of the vale contrast notably with the huge, smooth (and higher) Hameldon, opposite. From Widecombe village take the Bovey Tracey road and branch left beyond the river bridge (East Webburn) at the signpost 'Bonehill'. Notice the attractiveness of Bonehill, an ancient farming settlement of Dartmoor

longhouses. Arriving at Bonehill Gate, park (right) on Bonehill Lawn below Bonehill Rocks.

1 *Climb to Bonehill Rocks, a massive, weathered pile.*

2 *Follow the ridge north to Bel Tor.*

A Bel Tor offers the best and most detailed view of Widecombe village, truly reposing 'in-the-Moor'. The tor has interesting rock formations, including a rock corridor and several basins.

3 *Follow the ridge to Chinkwell Tor. A pointed rock-cluster on its south-west side is locally known as 'Sharp Tor'.*

4 *Follow the ridge to Honeybag Tor.*

B Honeybag Tor - 'Honeybags' as the moormen call it - although 100 ft (30 m) less in elevation than

Chinkwell, is indisputably sovereign of the range. On the steep hill west of the summit are several detached core-piles, indicating its former stature. Horizontal jointings and vertical partings are immense, as though a race of giants had assembled here to 'build' a tor and 'pave' the summit with granite bedding.

5 *Follow a green way threading through the bracken under the south side of the tor, down to a stony road.*

C Thornhill Lane is the ancient road from the Saxon Natsworthy settlements (at the head of the vale) to the old stannary and wool town of Ashburton, and passes between Bonehill Gate and the tors above. You will reach it beneath the toppled masses of Honeybag Tor; beyond Bonehill Lawn it passes by the ancient farms of Northway and Tunhill to reach the south-east escarpment under Buckland Beacon and Auswell Rocks, from where it descends to Ashburton on the line of the modern road. Notice below Chinkwell Tor the cone of Sharp Tor - less noticeable at close quarters - and, under Bel Tor, the huge, gaping slots produced by horizontal weathering in a small detached pile. The southward walk along Thornhill Lane is wholly delightful, allowing easy study of the changing aspects of the Widecombe vale, as well as appreciation of the scale of the southern hill-chain, which spans the vale's entire visual width.

6 *Parked cars on Bonehill Lawn come into view well before the road reaches them.*

45

RYDER

6 miles (9.6 km) Fairly strenuous; 750 ft (229 m) climb from moorgate

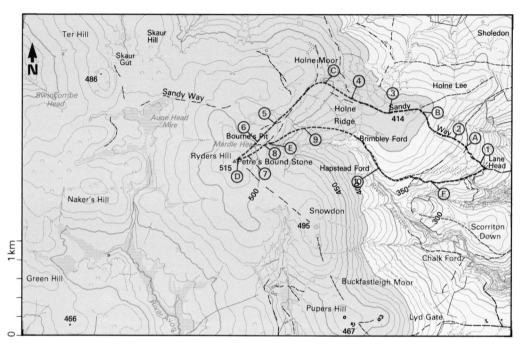

High places hold a fascination for most people, but do not attempt this walk in misty conditions. On southern Dartmoor the lonely dome of 'Ryder', as the moormen call Ryders Hill (highest land in the south), rises above the surrounding peatlands and gives tremendous views. To reach it is an achievement. From Holne village (west of Ashburton) take the narrow road to Michelcombe; drive through the hamlet and park near the sign prohibiting unauthorised vehicles from proceeding. A walk up the gently rising lane of just over half a mile (0.8 km) will bring you to Lanehead Gate.

1 *Pass through the gateway and follow the grass track directly ahead. Cross the dry channel of the Wheal Emma leat and pause for breath - and the view.*

A The border-country scene enfolds the Dart valley and Buckfast Abbey tower, and the little hills so typical of the South Devon landscape provide countless undulations declining to the distant estuary of the River Teign. The Moor's eastern highlands rise to the left, while on the right are the twin valleys of Holy Brook and Mardle, overlooked by the stern outlines of Pupers and Snowdon - the latter a lofty, east-facing down so named because snow tends to lie there for long in the Spring.

2 *Continue to ascend past a reave, another disused leat, and a thorn tree to a hilltop plain near tinners' mounds.*

B The track curves westward here and passes two bond-stones; both are inscribed 'PUDC' (the Venford reservoir catchment area for Paignton RDC) and RDH (Rural District of Holne); much of the central basin can be seen and the crest of Holne Ridge appears right.

3 *Ascend past another thorn tree at the head of a mining gert. Stay on the main path and pass well to the left of the next pair of bond-stones.*

4 *Higher again, a bond-stone appears on the left side of the track; the next*
Over

one is visible on the (false) crest ahead. Here leave the track and make (left) for mining mounds on the hilltop plain beyond.

C Viewpoint: a large expanse of east and south Devon is visible, and the desolate summit of Ryder rises in the south-east.

5 *Walk towards a deep gully (the Mardle valley-head) under the west flank of Snowdon.*

6 *Cross the gully and follow a clear, green path on Ryder's north-east slope. It passes another group of mining mounds, where a pit contains a 'B' bond-stone (Buckfastleigh Moor) and a nearby reave an 'H' stone (Holne Moor). The principal heights of southern Dartmoor appear as you climb, Eastern Whitaburrow first. The summit of Ryder soon comes in sight ahead.*

D Ryder. The summit is marked by an OS triangulation pillar and two bond-stones, one bearing 'H' (Holne) and the other 'B' (Buckfastleigh and Brent Moors). Views are far-reaching: the moorscape, too vast to be detailed, reaches across the valleys cleaving the north rim of the central basin to Vur Tor, Cut Hill, and Cosdon (15 miles/24 km away). Three Burrows, the disused Red Lake clay works and the Whitaburrow ridge are seen in the south, a view bordered by a long, gleaming line of English Channel.

7 *Several paths radiate north-east from Ryder; take the one pointing to Rippen Tor - highest point of the eastern highlands (to the right of Hey Tor's twin bosses).*

8 *On reaching the mining pits (Note 6), descend beside the gully to its foot.*

E This hidden hollow, containing the headsprings of the River Mardle, is Bourne's Pit. Bourne's Pit Stone stands in the hollow, bearing a large 'H' (Holne) and leaning some 45 degrees from the vertical.

9 *Follow the path (left) from Bourne's Pit Stone rounding the Mardle valley-head, to avoid the valley-floor mire. The sound of the infant river is audible and two picturesque fording places appear.*

10 *Join a track coming up from Hapstead Ford and rounding the hill contour; notice the bold prows of Snowdon and Pupers beyond the river.*

F Viewpoint. Between the two streams, Holy Brook and Mardle, rises the pleasant little mound of Scorriton Down, overshadowed by the giant hills above. The countryside now spread at your feet is of exceptional beauty - some of the best South Devon can offer. Beyond a leat (again the Wheal Emma) where a clapper footbridge can be seen, the path reaches Lanehead Gate in half a mile (0.8 km).

STALDON (pronounced 'Stahldon')

5 miles (8 km) Moderately easy; gradual climb 405 ft (137 m); dry

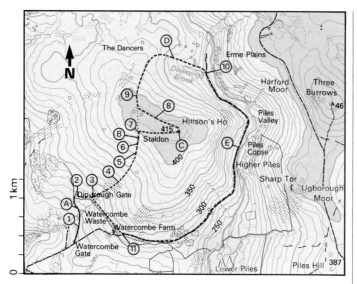

The massive hill of Staldon forms the west side of the deep Erme valley, over which, and southward to the sea, there are excellent views. The hill is topped by a Bronze Age cairn, with one of the most effectively sited stone rows in Europe nearby. Drive north from Cornwood to Vicarage Bridge over the River Yealm. Cross; turn right. Take the first turning left, between houses, then immediately right. Drive through Watercombe Waste Gate and park away from the tracks. The notice 'Permitted Path to the Moor' means that no rights of way and parking exist, but that the farmer owning the Waste permits both to considerate visitors who close gates and leave no litter.

1 *Follow the track through -*

A Watercombe Waste. The ancient track, beside which flows the Blachford leat, is overshadowed by -hollies, oaks, ashes, elms and beeches. The leat flows from Redaven Lake at the ford. Beyond it, left, is Dip-trough Gate and the old Watercombe sheep dip.

2 *Beyond Dip-trough Gate leave the track and follow the wall of the Waste, right.*

3 *At the wall-corner walk up the wide, shallow Redaven Gulf past a small rockfield and above it, another wider one.*

4 *When the rockfield becomes dense you will see above left the lower end of Staldon Row.*

5 *Make for the lowest, massive terminal stone of the row.*

6 *Follow the row.*

B Staldon Stone Row. The dramatic effect of this row on the hillcrest can be seen from the hills east of the Erme valley. On the row's east side there is an intermediate grave and near the fifth to the end stone on the west side a remnant kisvaen and another grave.

7 *Leave the row at the intermediate kistvaen and cross the moor (right) in line with the cairn-crowned dome of Three Burrows; the highest hill of the further valley-side range. Walk towards large stone cairn ahead.*

C Staldon Burrow and Hillson's House. The angular appearance of this large Bronze Age cairn is due to the enterprising, if eccentric behaviour of a clock-maker recluse, named Hillson. He retreated here in the early 1800s, built the house and made eight-day clocks.

8 *From Hillson's House, return to the stone row by making (right) for the tallest stones.*

9 *From the end of the row descend the hill due north and pass round the contour (left) of a tributary valley-head, to walk down -*

D Downing's Brook valley. Near where this swift little stream meets the Erme, on the left bank is a fine example of a Dartmoor medieval tinners' cache. Built entirely of stone corbelling, with a domed roof, of a type known as a 'beehive hut'.

10 *A stony track crosses Downing's Brook in a dip below the beehive hut.*

E Piles Copse. Seen from the Erme valley floor is this huge canopy of oaks on the opposite, steep hillside under Sharp Tor, one of the primeval oak groves unique to Dartmoor.

11 *When the track reaches the Waterworks gate, leave it and walk over the moor (right) beside the enclosure wall. Cross Redaven Lake, return to the start at Dip-trough Gate.*

Walk 26

HEY TOR, QUARRIES AND GRANITE TRAMROAD

2½ miles (4 km) Very easy; dry

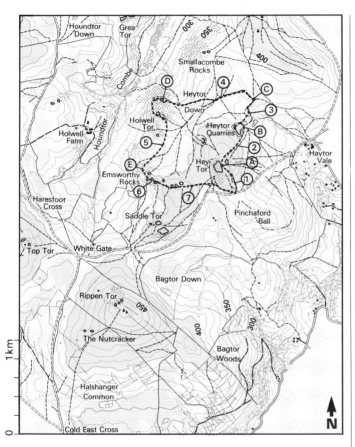

high wind. Stand below the east pile's immense rock-wall where trial holes have been drilled in the granite.

2 *Follow a path directly in front of the rock-wall, descending through heather to the corner of a wire fence; notice the line of the tramroad on the flank of Heytor Down ahead. Descend and enter the quarry.*

B Heytor Quarry. The harshness of the quarry face is softened by heather and gorse, which in high summer is extremely colourful on the surrounding moorland, and by the water of Heytor Ponds. Notice the remaining wooden beam and iron winch of the crane.

3 *Follow the tramroad track from the quarry (granite rail sets will soon appear in the turf) to a set of junction 'points'.*

4 *Follow the main line westward (left), through a shallow cutting and down to its terminus -*

D Holwell Quarry. A sheer working face, a crane-base and ruined buildings speak of intense industry here 160 years ago. Climb Holwell Tor above the quarry and look over Houndtor Combe to Grea Tor and Great Hound Tor.

5 *Cross a hollow in the hillside towards -*

E Emsworthy Rocks. Here are two more quarries of the Heytor complex, one at either end of a long rock-ridge where branch lines of the railroads terminate.

6 *Follow the crest of the Emsworthy rock-ridge and notice the second quarry.*

7 *Follow a green path joining the Bovey Tracey road at Heytor car park.*

The huge granite bosses of High ('Hey' in the vernacular) Tor, are a notable landmark from the sea, moorland and the east Devon heathlands. Easy to reach it is a popular tor with tourists. Below it on the north side are the quarries from which granite was extracted in 1825 for the foundation stone of London Bridge. This travelled in horse-drawn trucks down the unique granite tramroad to the Stover Canal for shipment at Teignmouth Quay; a milestone in Dartmoor's industrial history. Take the Bovey Tracey-Widecombe road to the car park south of the road on the crest of Heytor Down.

1 *Follow the broad path to the tor.*

A Hey Tor has a large rock basin reached by steps cut in the rock of the east pile; do not use them in a

---

49

KES TOR, SCORHILL GORGE
2 miles (3.2 km) Easy; dry

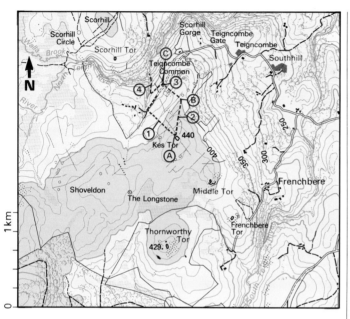

Kes Tor, a fine mass of cohesive granite on the Moor's north-east escarpment, is another landmark visible from afar, and the best place from which to study the great middle reach basin of the North Teign River. South of the tor the escarpment is marked by Middle, Frenchbere and Thornworthy Tors. On its east slopes - Teigncombe Common - are the homes and fields of Celtic peoples of the Iron Age, and rising to its summit is the sound of North Teign in Scorhill Gorge. From Chagford follow signs to Kes Tor. Beyond Teigncombe (third of three hamlets) a short rise brings you to Teigncombe Gate (cattle grid). The road beyond, ending at Batworthy, passes a massive pound with hut circle, right; park on the moorside (right) beyond this.

1 *Ascend to the tor; the best path is opposite Batworthy Bridge.*

A Kes Tor's striking character results from its vertical compactness. There are several summit rock basins, including the largest on Dartmoor. Views across the Teign basin are splendid.

B Many huts of the once large Iron Age village have been overplanted in the nearby enclosures, but 27 remain on the open common, some well over 35 ft (10.5 m) in diameter 'with walls three to four and a half feet (0.9-1.4 m) thick faced internally with large vertical slabs'! Two droveways for stock run between the fields. Alongside the upper droveway is a square enclosure for impounding animals.

3 *Cross the Teigncombe Gate-Batworthy road towards the massive hut circle at the roadside near the car parking space.*

C Roundy Pound is of such size and Iron Age sophistication as to be identifiable as the village chieftan's residence. Furthermore, iron smelting was found by Lady Fox to have taken place in the hut. There are separate rooms, a kitchen drain, and a doorway leading to the lower droveway towards Batworthy Brook. The hut has an internal diameter of 37 ft (11 m) and is enclosed by a private pound divided into segments by radial walls, and containing a small hut at the northeast corner. It is rewarding to visualise the scene here 2500 years ago: a village of perhaps 40-50 thatched huts emitting wood and peat smoke from their conical roofs, beasts being prodded along droveways, children playing, the sound of the river rushing through Scorhill Gorge, and the environment of majestic moorland much as it appears today.

4 *Follow the wide lower droveway to its open end above Batworthy Brook; follow the brook to its meeting with the river. Scorhill Gorge, although not very deep, is narrow enough to confine the river, when in spate, with sensational results.*

Reference
[1] Fox, Lady Aileen, 1954. Report for the University of Exeter on the excavation of the Roundy Pound site. *Transactions of the Devonshire Association*, Vol 86.

Walk 28
GER TOR AND TAVY CLEAVE
3½ miles (5.6 km) Some rough, wet ground; 450 ft (137 m) climb from start

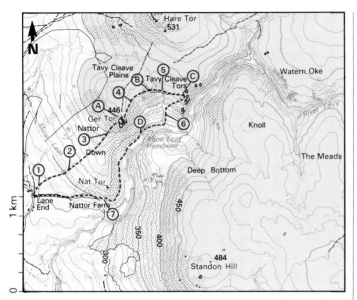

The area lies in the Willsworthy live-firing range, where firing is frequent, except during August; check the firing programme before setting out. West Dartmoor's Tavy is the second swiftest river in Britain, second only that is, to Spey in the Cairngorms, Scotland. Its swift current is due to it making a descent of 1000 ft (305 m) in only eight miles (12.8 km). Tavy has cut a rugged, impressive gorge over the ages; treeless and rockbound, it is known as Tavy Cleave. From the A386 Tavistock-Okehampton road turn right at Mary Tavy War Memorial four and a quarter miles (6.8 km) from Tavistock then take the first left turning, signposted 'HORNDON' and continue to Lane End (where the tarmac road ends); cross the cattle grid and park on open ground near the military flagpole. Do not obstruct any track.

1 *Walk towards Ger Tor, at the head of Nattor Down.*

2 *Cross the Mine leat bridge; (the leat once supplied the water-wheels of a large copper mine at Mary Tavy, but now runs to Kingsett Down hydroelectric plant).*

3 *Remain on the track until near the hill-crest, then make for a clear, grassy patch near rocks ahead.*

A View from upper, north-west side of tor: this possesses a grandeur not common on British moorlands. Below, Tavy leaves its cleave with an audible roar, Vur Tor and the ridges of the northern fen appear in the east, and Standon raises its bulk beyond the river.

4 *Cross the tract of level ground towards Hare Tor's summit cone; this is*

Tavy Cleave Plains. When near the stones of a hut village below, right; descend to it.

B The first hut, right, has original door jambs and a step into the interior (floor then was at least 2 ft (0.6 m) lower). Cross the village towards Sharp Tor above the rock-ridge ahead and visit another hut with exceptionally good door jambs. Stand within the doorway and appreciate the wonderful prospect.

5 *Make for the ford in the tributary valley ahead; the path continues to a wide gap in the rocks of Sharp Tor. Avoid the gap and bear right to a cleft in the middle of the main pile.*

C On reaching 'Tavy Cleave Sharp' walk close under the rock and look through the cleft for the view.

6 *Descend to the main valley, by returning to the tributary ford and following the stream downwards. Although difficult in places, this is not to be compared with the ground that would be encountered in a direct walk from Sharp Tor to the river.*

D The Mine leat and its headweir are visible below. A rough path follows the river bank to the weir at the foot of the cleave; from the weir follow the leatside path, which eventually curves below the rocks of Nat Tor to cross Nattor Down.

7 *Leave the leat beyond the bend and follow a grass path down to the entrance gate of Nattor farm (left), then take the farm road to Lane End and the start.*

SCORHILL CIRCLE, SHOVELDON
3½ miles (5.6 km) Easy; dry

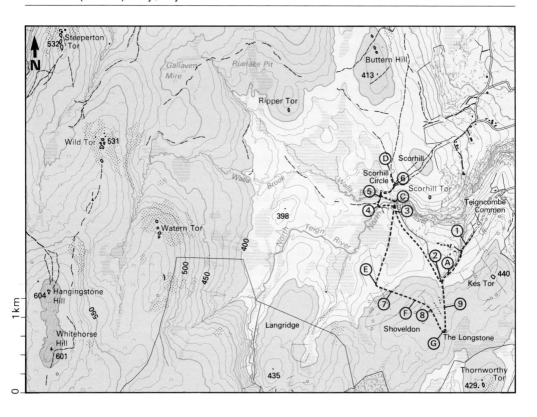

The north-east edge of the high moor, known generally as the 'Chagford area', is renowned for its beauty, enhanced by the lofty tors and hills on the west rim of the North Teign River's middle reach basin, the painter's paradise where Walla Brook and Teign meet, and the fascinating field of antiquities on Shoveldon. This walk of two to three hours, depending on how long you dally at the delectable Walla Brook Foot, is in itself a lesson in topography and archaeology, enhanced by the bracing air and sweet water of these high, north-eastern commons. Huge Cosdon, two and a half miles (4 km) north of Scorhill Circle, overlooks the entire scene, and the peace of it all lies in the nine wild and rugged miles (14.4 km) between Batworthy Corner and the next nearest road at Lydford in the west. From Chagford follow signs to Kes Tor. Beyond Teigncombe (third of three hamlets) a short rise brings you to Teigncombe Gate (cattle grid). The road beyond, ending at Batworthy, passes a massive pound with hut circle, right; park on the moorside (right) beyond this.

1 *Walk to Batworthy Bridge and follow the stony track ahead.*

A The strange granite object near the head-mire of Batworthy Brook is 'Cow Bridge' and the incised 'G' on the slab indicates a boundary of Gidleigh parish.

2 *At Batworthy Corner follow the path near the wall, right.*

B Viewpoint: topping a slight rise ahead, pause. Whitehorse and Hangingstone Hills (at almost
Over

2000 ft/610 m) rim the Teign basin in the west, highest points on a hill-chain continuing northward to Wild Tor, Steeperton Tor and Cosdon. Ahead are the standing stones of Scorhill Circle.

3 *Diverge from the wall when it descends to the river; cross (North Teign) on a crude, makeshift clapper bridge (replacing one swept away by a flood in 1826).*

4 *Turn left and walk up the peninsula to the more attractive clapper spanning Walla Brook. Cross; turn right and return down the peninsula to an unusual boulder in the river below the confluence of the streams.*

C The Tolmen, or 'holed stone', is entirely the natural result of water-erosion, a pothole excavated in a past age when the river level was higher. A Dartmoor tradition challenges the visitor to pass through the hole, while making a wish, and emerge dryshod on the river bank. Notice that the boulder has several rock basins - the formative origin of the Tolmen.

5 *Return to the bridge and turn into the track (right); this crosses the (flowing)*

Gidleigh leat on a cart clapper bridge and leads to the stone circle.

D Scorhill Circle is a fine example of what may be termed a Bronze Age 'temple': 23 stones remain erect, the tallest eight feet, two inches (2.5 km) in height, of an original stand of 65-70, with a diameter of 88 ft (27 m). You will appreciate the setting in which the monument stands.

6 *Return to the Walla Brook bridge; cross both streams, walk southward over Batworthy Common, diverging from the wall (left) and making for the crest of the down (Shoveldon) ahead. Keep well above Batworthy Inner Mire (below, right). Look for a nearby conspicuous reave between down and river. Near it, at the foot of the down, make for two prominent standing stones.*

E The stones are the remains of a dolmen (Neolithic burial chamber) which probably stood seven to nine feet (2.0-2.7 m) above the ground. Within view from here are the stones of the nearest of the Shoveldon rows.

7 *Wander along the rows at will; three*

are well-defined and remains exist of two more.

F Each row commences at a grave (once a kistvaen) at its higher end; that heading the north-easternmost row is enclosed by a rare fourfold circle. (See also Walk 1).

8 *Walk south 250 yds (229 m) from the highest grave (on the crest of the down) to a tall standing stone, noticing, right, a field system and hut circle.*

G The menhir, known as the 'Longstone', terminates a short double row without a discernible grave; letters incised on the stone are 'C' (Chagford), 'G' (Gidleigh), and 'DC' (Duchy of Cornwall), indicating the meeting places of those parishes with the Forest of Dartmoor. Noticeable from here is the poised logan stone on the west slope of Thornworthy Tor, and glint of Fernworthy reservoir in the South Teign valley.

9 *Return northward over the hillcrest, follow the north-east stone row to Batworthy Corner, and so to the start.*

Walk 30
CRANMERE POOL
3½ miles (5.6 km) Terrain moderate to rough; very wet at times

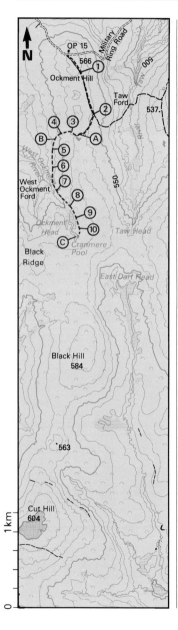

This area lies within the Okehampton live-firing range; check the firing programme before setting out. At the head of the West Ockment River on north Dartmoor is a large depression in the peat bog, roughly ovoid in shape. It contained standing water until the early 1840s, when an outlet was dug in the north bank to drain the pool. Samuel Rowe, in his *A Perambulation of Dartmoor* (1848) tells us that the bank was breached by a shepherd, several of whose sheep had drowned in the pool. In 1854, James Perrott, a Dartmoor guide of Chagford, placed a glass container within a stone cairn on the drained bed of the pool and issued a challenge to intrepid visitors to deposit their cards in the glass jar as proof of successful search for the elusive hollow. A tin box succeeded the glass jar in 1889, a post box with a visitors' book in 1912 and new replacements followed between the two World Wars, thus the early trickle of Cranmere explorers has today become almost a procession. The former presence of the heron at the pool accounts for its name - 'Crane Mere'; today it is not uncommon to see, in addition to foot-marks, the tracks of fox and otter on the damp peat floor of the pool. The great majority of walkers - by no means all succeeding in their venture - knowing nothing of an easier route, beeline across the fen by aligning recognisable points and optimistically setting out. The route given here is in part an ancient one, for the moormen needed to visit the pool long before it became the

modern custom to search it out and deposit mail in the box. You should take postcards or writing paper on which to leave your message. This is an out-and-return one-way route: it is inadvisable, even during a dry summer, to take young children back by bee-lining - 'bog-hopping' as it is called - over the fen. WARNING: Do not attempt this walk in misty weather. From Okehampton drive to Moorgate at the Battle Camp. Take the military ring-road, open to the public on non-firing days, cross Moor Brook and fork right at the junction three quarters of a mile (1.2 km) from Moorgate. Drive a further three miles (4.8 km) to the summit of Ockment Hill and park near a military observation post (OP 15) beside the road. Views from here over the north moor are very fine.

1 *Walk south along the stony road for half a mile (0.8 km) to a turning space for military vehicles.*

2 *Branch right from the road into a green track leading to a peaty pool.*

A Viewpoint: Huggaton Pool. The high tops of the fen are seen (left) rising to an apex at Cut Hill. Ahead is the long ridge of Amicombe Hill and, right, the High Willes-Yes Tor ridge. In the foreground the land declines to the upper reach of the West Ockment River.

3 *From Huggaton Pool walk north-west (right) and enter an opening in a peat bank. A narrow footpath exists, and marker-stones have been laid on the bank where the path enters a cutting: this is the peat pass known as -*   *Over*

54

4 *Huggaton Cut. It soon becomes deeper and, although often very wet underfoot, will guide you safely through the fen to within sight of the infant River Ockment.*

B Upper West Ockment valley: this is as wild a place as any on a British moorland. The castle-like rocks of Great Links Tor appear above Amicombe Hill, ahead, High Willes is still seen (right), while closing in on every side is the jagged, fissured terrain of the northern fen. Next comes the most tricky part of the route. As the peat pass ends (in a wet, rush-covered floor) there is a small set stone on the north (right) side as well as a small pile of stones on the edge of a grass bank, left. Two or three paths lead away from the pass; take the one (left) which keeps fairly high above the valley but always below the black edge of the peat.

5 *Follow the path to a wide, shallow,* green gully: it enters the higher end and leaves from the lower beside a large bed of rushes.

6 *You now begin to converge with the river - but set your direction on the tributary valley pointing towards you on the far side of the river. Stay well above the river until the path clearly leads down to it at -*

7 *West Ockment Ford; the stream in the tributary valley you have been aiming for, here joins the river. Turn left and ascend beside the river, now passing through a short hole.*

8 *At the head of the hole follow the well-marked path diverging (left) from the river and running ahead through a wide, grassy valley. The path stays near the edge of the peat (left) throughout.*

9 *At the valley head, the path curves towards the headsprings of the river situated in a treacherous, boggy hole. It then veers to climb a high peat bank ahead.*

10 *From the inside edge of the peat bank, look down upon the hollow of your destination.*

C Cranmere Pool. The shape of the former tarn, and the post box now in the (west) bank, are at once visible. Hangingstone Hill and Great Kneeset are equidistant, respectively east and west. High Willes and Amicombe remain in view, while the inhospitable height of Cut Hill lifts its fen-covered slopes above the surrounding sea of fen - 20 square miles (51.8 sq km) in extent. Sign the visitors' book, frank and deposit your mail, remove mail already there (deposited previous to the day of your walk) and depart. On the return walk, do not fail to turn into the wide, rush-filled gully (Note 5), well beyond and above the river - and keep a sharp eye open for that elusive set stone at the foot of Huggaton Cut.

TAW PLAIN AND THE BELSTONE RANGE

2½ miles (4 km) Fairly easy; dry; some rocky stretches

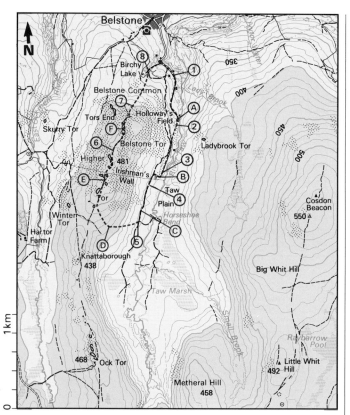

The southern portion of this walk is within the Okehampton military firing range, therefore check the firing programme before setting out.

The scene on Taw Plain could only be Dartmoor. Tors and hills, folded one against another into the misty distance, surround a huge amphitheatre, its floor 1000 ft (305 m) above sea level. It is rugged scenery at its best. Dartmoor sends only two main rivers, Taw and Ockment, to the Bristol Channel coast. Taw is the longer and has its own estuary beginning at the ancient borough and port of Barnstaple. Drive to the village of Belstone, leaving either from Sticklepath or Tongue End (both are on the A30 road). Parking space at Birchy Lake Gate, which is a little further on, is very limited and it is advisable to park beside the road on Belstone Green and walk to the moorgate.

1 *Walk downhill (right) to* Lower *Birchy Lake Gate. Follow the rough* track past Bernard's Acre to Holloway's Field at the riverside.

A The strange mixture here of modern alloy metals, concrete and a rustic granite fireplace is the result of modernising an ancient sheep-dip adjoining a granite mason's yard and forge. The leaps and bounds of the river here are quite beautiful.

2 *Pass through the two gateways at the dip and walk upstream. The small rockpile, above left, is Ladyback Tor.*

3 *On reaching a small water-works building and weir, mount steps (right) in the bank to Taw Plain.*

B Viewpoint: Steeperton Tor rises ahead; Little Whit Hill, left; Ock Tor half-right, and the Belstone range immediately above (right).

4 *Turn left into a sandy path; several hatch covers here conceal an underground pumping station.*

C Again study the view, for the distant hills seem to change position as you walk: they are (left to right) - Cosdon, Big Whit Hill, Round Tor, Metheral Hill, Wild Tor, Steeperton·Hill and Tor, Ockment Hill, Ock Tor; Small Brook and Steeperton Brook drop through deep valleys to join Taw, the two last peninsulating Steeperton Hill. Taw Plain was a primeval lake-bed and retains a sufficient subterranean water-table to justify the pumping works to supply North Devon.

5 *Join a hard track coming out from Birchy Lake and branching to a picturesque ford on the river known as 'First Crossing Place'. Leave the track opposite the branch to the ford and climb the hill, right, to Higher Tor; ease the climb by zig-zagging.*

Over

D Hillside viewpoint: Ock Tor is nearest; on the valley floor, strips of shining water indicate Taw Marsh, the drier terrain of Taw Plain continuing east of the river. The grassy tumps (nearer than Ock Tor) are named Knattaborough. In the distance between Steeperton and Ock Tors is the remote Hangingstone Hill (1983 ft/604 m), the fourth highest of the Dartmoor hills.

E Higher Tor. There are three piles, the lower ones being satellites of the upper; all have striking features, such as rock 'walls' and huge clitters, and give wonderful westerly views: on the extreme edge of the Moor, right to left, the three grassy hills are East Hill, Halstock, Black Down; the four tors are, in ascending order, Rough, West Mil, Yes and High Willes. In the East Ockment valley below are the enclosures and farmhouse of Hartor Farm - the setting for Eden Phillpott's gripping tale, *The Secret Woman*. Several tracks are seen, two of them forming the military ringroad, and the glistening waterfall in the centre is Blackaven Brook passing through Hartor Hole. The amazing stone wall rushing up to the summit of the tor and down the other side is the relic of a 19th century attempt at common land piracy; the labourers employed were Irishmen, the wall having ever since been known as Irishman's Wall. This ill-conceived plan was thwarted by the muscular intervention of the commoners of Belstone.

6 *Follow the ridge to -*

F Belstone Tor. Views from here of Taw Plain and Marsh are very fine; Watern Tor (North Teign country) is visible on the south horizon (left of Hangingstone Hill), as is the summit cairn on Cosdon. The rockpile below, left, is appropriately named Tors' End; the wooded gorge of East Ockment, West Cleave, lies beyond, while the northward view stretches across the North Hams to Exmoor's edge.

7 *Descend in line with the hill slope sweeping upward to the right of Belstone; this will lead you into a clitter-free path. The rocky side of Belstone Cleave (the granite gorge of Taw) will come in sight, and the houses and church of Belstone village are to the left. Make for the lowest placed, inner corner of the newtake below, where* Higher *Birchy Lake Gate is situated.*

8 *Pass through the gateway and return to the start.*

Walk 32

WHIT TOR AND LANGSTONE MOOR

4½ miles (7.2 km) Moderately easy; dry; gradual climb of 650 ft (198 m)

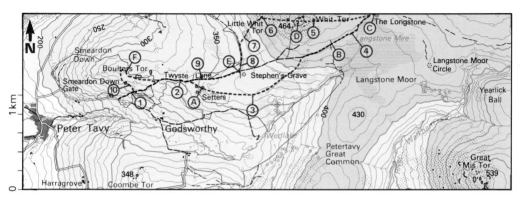

WARNING: the eastern extremity of this walk is within the Merrivale military firing range, therefore check the firing programme before setting out.

Western Dartmoor has an aura of stern aloofness absent from the gentler south and the more visited eastern moor: vast tracts of grass moor, much of it heatherless, extensive fields of jagged border-rock, lofty tors of mountainous proportions rise between the rapid Tavy and Walkham rivers.

Take the A386 road north from Tavistock; four and a quarter miles (6.8 km) from the town, branch right to the village of Peter Tavy from which the writer takes his name. Beyond the church, turn right to Smeardon Down Gate. Keep left at a fork-roads and park near a notice requesting 'Please Park Here'.

1 *Ascend the steep track; the largest tors of upper Walkham country appear, right. Boulters Tor is nearby, left, and at the top of the rise Whit Tor is ahead.*

2 *The portion of wall-bordered track is Twyste Lane. Beyond it on the right is a small rockpile. Walk across to it.*

A Setters (Rocks). Viewpoint: west - Kit Hill (the minestack hill) and Bodmin Moor; south-west - Tavistock town in the vale of Tavy; south-east - the Walkham tors; below - Higher and Lower Godsworthy Farms in the Wedlake valley.

3 *Cross the moor above the Wedlake enclosures, right; at a striped range-pole, bear half-left and return to the ascending track.*

B From the crest of the down notice the widespread, treacherous Langstone Mire (right) source of Wed Lake; beyond it are seen the dark stones of Langstone Moor circle.

4 *Follow the track ahead to the menhir.*

C Langstone Moor antiquities. The menhir was damaged by American troops during World War II manoeuvres. It is the terminal of a now remnant stone row running from a ruined grave 110 yds (101 m) away. Its Dartmoor name, the lang- or long-stone, is attached to both

mire and moor in this area. The stone circle mentioned was similarly damaged; it has a diameter of 60 ft (18.3 m) and although in itself not very striking, is scenically enhanced by its background, Great Mis Tor. Its setting can be appreciated from the Longstone.

5 *Walk directly from the Longstone to the tor.*

D Whit Tor - an extraordinary wilderness of jagged masses of the border-rock known as epidiotite. A large spread of north Dartmoor is visible, including Vur Tor and Cut Hill. On approaching the broken central pile, notice a stone rampart, once large, now crumbling, which actually encircles the hilltop. This is part of an Iron Age fort, built apparently for the safe refuge of villagers from the plain below who, from time to time, expected to come under attack by raiders. Views southeastward also are good and include North Hessary Tor, the Plym ridge, Lether and Sharp Tors and Peak Hill.

6 *Walk to Little Whit Tor, a pile with*
Over

58

a markedly jagged crest and an inner 'court', or clearing. Other, smaller rockpiles also rise from the hill.

7 *Descend the down between two large areas of clitter towards a newtake wall. Cross a rectangular Iron Age enclosure with hut circles: more huts exist nearby on the down, constituting the village mentioned above. Mary Tavy church tower and Gibbet Hill are clearly seen from here.*

8 *Walk to the newtake corner, left, and continue to a standing stone beside the Langstone Moor track.*

E At this desolate spot, the stone, known as Stephen's Grave, marks the burial in 1762 of a suicide - a victim of unrequited love.

9 *Follow the track westward. After passing through Twyste Lane (Note 2) leave the track and follow the wall, right - an excellent example of*

a cornditch wall; the ditch is clear and the height of the expertly built wall obviated the need for a top - coping. It will guide you to -

F Boulters Tor - more craggy masses of the Whit Tor type, giving fine views of the western border-country.

10 *Take the path (southeast) through the bracken field leading to a green plain and the track. Turn right into this and descend to the start.*

PEN BEACON AND SHIEL TOP

4½ miles (7.2 km) Terrain easy; gradual climb 800 ft (244 m)

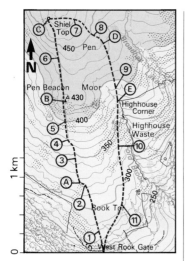

Pen Beacon is probably the only place in England that overlooks the estuarine valleys of six rivers - the water seen gleaming in four of them as they approach the broad, shining band of the English Channel. For this walk try to choose a day of atmospheric clarity as the views are panoramic. Here the eye can range from the historic River Dart in the southeast to Tamar in the west, the river separating Cornwall from Devon - or from England, as the Cornish have it. From this remarkable place, news has been flashed by fire over the centuries, and on a summer's day in 1588 men stood with torches at the ready to light a great signal beacon, first in a long chain; soon, all England knew the Spanish Armada had been sighted. Henry Newbolt, in his poem *Drake's Drum,* gives these words to the spirit of the Armada's vanquisher:

'When the Dons sight Devon,
    I'll quit the port of Heaven, and
Drum them up the Channel as
    we drummed them long ago.'
Take the Yelverton-Cornwood road; from Cornwood, proceed north towards Dartmoor. Take first left and follow road for one mile (1.6 km) past East Rook farm. Travel straight on at a road junction and park at end of tarmac road. Walk up track to East Rook Gate and on to edge of moor. Then follow wall on left for 400 yds (366 m) to reach West Rook Gate.

1 *Ignore stony tracks right and left (beside cornditch walls) and take the steep grass path directly ahead. The sound of machinery at the nearby clay works will be with you for some time. Pass through a rockfield and Pen Beacon will appear ahead.*

2 *Bear left to the remains of Rook Tor; notice the remaining segment of a hut circle; cross a dry leat channel.*

A Rook Tor, a ruined pile with scarcely one rock upon another. The rockfield (Note 1) is part of the tor's clitter; there are pleasing views over Plymouth Sound, the Hamoaze (the entry to Devonport at the mouth of Tamar) and numerous villages in the South Hams.

3 *Ascend direct to Pen Beacon. Cross the leat, used until World War II and which ran from Broadall Head to the Cholwich Town clay works, below and to the left.*

4 *When a green strip is seen on the hillslope ahead, bear left to a nearby group of rocks; here runs the Pen Moor reave from Rook Tor via the green strip ahead to Pen Beacon and Shiel Top - probably marking a medieval manor boundary.*

5 *Views become extensive as you climb; aim for the left side of a conspicuous boulder on the hill-crest, and the summit cairn will come into sight.*

B Pen Beacon The view is worth detailed study: Cornwall's St Austell and Bodmin Moors form the background to the Tamar valley; nearer are Plymouth and Devonport Dockyard where cranes, and at times, warships, are visible; 500ft (152 m) below is the largest china clay pit in the world, part of the huge workings on Lee Moor of English China Clays. The stones of the summit cairn have been used to build a small marker cairn, a shelter-wall and a nearby look-out hut, and an OS triangulation post stands nearby.

6 *Ascend northward beside the reave to a diminutive tor -*

C Shiel Top The rock was once enclosed by a prehistoric cairn, a practice found elsewhere on Dartmoor. View: Yelverton village is backed by the higher Walkham tors; in the distant north are Vur Tor, Cut and Hangingstone Hills, and Siddaford Tor. Another OS triangulation post stands on higher ground nearby.

7 *Follow a narrow path east to a large, flat rock. Notice the slot-marks of stone-cutting on many boulders.*

8 *From the flat rock, change direction southeast to reach a wall (below, right).*

D Viewpoint: the large, shallow hollow seen (left) is Broadall Head, source of a tributary of the River Yealm. Eastern Whitaburrow,

Over

Three Burrows and Sharp Tor are visible on the skyline.

9 *Descend to the lower wall corner at Highhouse Ford on Ford Brook.*

E Viewpoint: the border-country lies spread below, warmed in winter by the southern sun, its rays reflected by the lowland reaches of the Dartmoor rivers.

10 *Descend southward towards the roofs of Cornwood - the village nearest the Moor. The wooded valley below, left, is that of Yealm.*

11 *On reaching the hill-spur, bear left to the hollow containing West Rook Gate. Descend to the start.*

Walk 34

THREE FRONTIER TORS

5½ miles (8.8 km) Moderately easy; mostly dry; initial climb of 500 ft (152 m)

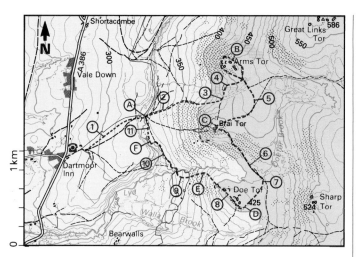

The west escarpment of Dartmoor consists of a double rampart of tors extending between the Rivers West Ockment and Tavy. Sourton Tors, Great Noddon, Arms Tor, Brai and Doe Tors rise steeply above the border-country at their feet, from where they present an impressive appearance. On attaining any one of these summits, however, a greater range of tors and hills is seen beyond, one of which, Great Links Tor looks out to both seas peninsulating the land - the English and Bristol Channels. It is wild, rocky country to which the River Lyd provides a softening touch.

Take the A386 road north from Tavistock (or south from Okehampton) to the Dartmoor Inn, Lydford. Turn into a lane leading to Dartmoor Gate. Vehicles can cause erosion. Please park near gate and do not drive across the Down.

1 *Follow the track beside the cornditch wall, left, to the river.*

A High Down Ford is picturesque, with fine stepping stones and a wooden footbridge; the mound of Great Noddon rises upstream, Brai Tor is ahead between Arms and Doe Tors, and the 'second rampart' Hare Tor dominates the background.

2 *Cross the river and take the green track directly ahead mounting to the Arms-Brai col.*

3 *On reaching an enclosure (only the posts remain) leave the track and make left for Arms Tor: a bad mire lies on the hillside below.*

4 *Follow the line of posts at the lower enclosure corner; the ground is wet, but passable. The tor is now seen to consist of several piles - even more will appear on gaining the summit.*

B Arms Tor's summit plateau is scattered with the cores and remains of several piles. The main (west) pile heads a rock-ridge, and the east pile, grotesquely broken, has a rock basin on the summit. The view of the higher tor-range is very fine;

southward, Brai Tor and its cross are outlined against distant Plymouth Sound, and in the north, Lyd flows through a hidden valley under Great Noddon, backed by the Sourton Tors. The river bends westward to leave the Moor and penetrate a huge spread of west Devon, passing below Lydford Church and Castle and pointing towards the Tamar valley and Bodmin Moor.

5 *Follow a clear path across the plain, curving (right) to Brai Tor.*

C Brai Tor. Again - several piles, more cohesive than the Arms Tor granite. The 13 ft (4 m) granite cross surmounting the summit rock was erected by Dartmoor painter William Widgery in 1887 in honour of Queen Victoria's Golden Jubilee. Southward, Lyd is seen to enter a gorge under Black Rock and Doetor Brook to approach a scarp above its series of falls, while Doe Tor exemplifies a granite tor in extreme ruin and decay.

6 *Walk to the right of Sharp Tor to avoid the dense clitter on Brai Tor's south slope, then make for the valley at a point beyond which a green way ascends Doe Tor. Steep, heathery banks and the crystal-clear stream make this - Doetor Ford - a lovely place.*

7 *Follow the green way to the tor. Notice the military sign (right) - 'DO NOT PICK UP ANY METAL OBJECTS'.*

D Doe Tor. Under the east end of the tor is a tinners' cache formed by lowering a huge slab upon boulders and 'plugging' the side gaps with

Over

small stones. An ancient enclosure under the north side of the east pile was once used as a stock-pound. The lower, west pile is the more broken; below it, south-west, are the fields and ruins of Doetor Farm. Lydford Sharp and Hare Tors tower above it, and Doetor Brook flows through the steep 'Foxholes' valley.

8 *Walk towards the lower slope of Brai Tor, keeping the Doe Tor clitter to your left. Cross a flowing leat and a broken wall; about 100 yds (91 m) below this, leave the path and follow the brink of the valley (right).*

E Doetor Falls is a magical place in autumn: golden bracken, rowan trees laden with red berries, grey rocks, cascades, falls, pools, water-slides, and with Brai Tor Cross high above, it is an enchanting place at any time.

9 *Descend to Doetor Farm Ford; a modern bridge replaces a clapper destroyed by the brook in spate.*

10 *Follow the green track beyond the brook until opposite a crag on the further side of the Lyd valley; leave the track and follow a narrow path to the river bank.*

F Black Rock Falls, like many on the Dartmoor streams, consist of ledges rather than a precipitous cliff. The crag is of border-slate as the moorland granite ceases abruptly in midstream. The seat and plaque under Black Rock commemorate a young officer, killed in World War I, who had a particular love for the Moor.

11 *Follow the riverside path past the old Lydford village water-intake, cross the river at High Down Ford and return to the start.*

A RAILROAD WALK - PLYMOUTH & DARTMOOR RAILWAY: GWR

4½ miles (7.2 km) Moderately easy; some uneven grass moor

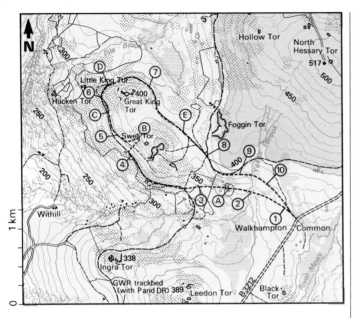

England's only mountain railway (Yelverton-Princetown) was closed by Dr Beeching in 1956. Built in 1881, it used most of the trackbed of an earlier line, the Plymouth & Dartmoor Railway (P & DR), a horse-truck tramroad (opened 1823) for transporting granite for shipment on the Plym estuary from Sir Thomas Tyrwhitt's quarries near Princetown. The serpentine, finely engineered track passes over rocky moorland and offers exceptional views over western Dartmoor. Take the Yelverton-Princetown road (B3212) for about one and a half miles (2.7 km) beyond Goadstone Pond. Park in the small disused quarry (left) near a right-hand bend.

1 *Walk towards the jagged quarry-head of Swell Tor.*

2 *Cross a flowing leat and descend to the valley of Yestor Brook among tin works; continue in the same direction to a Bronze Age village with associated pounds. The main enclosure wall has a paved north-east entrance; some huts have entrance passages and standing door jambs.*

A Viewpoint: southward rise Leedon Tor and Ingra Tor; the GWR trackbed runs below Ingra Tor. The deviating P & DR crosses the brook on an arch-bridge. The transition between moorland, border-country, lowlands, Tamar valley and east Cornwall seen from here, is very pleasing.

3 *The united railroad lines curve below the hut village. Walk through two broken walls (250 yds/229 m apart) to the rail track.*

4 *In a short way leave the rail track and walk to a row of large, shaped granite objects near Swell Tor.*

B Swell Tor Quarry supplied stone for several early 19th century London buildings, including Nelson's column and parts of London Bridge. The P & DR siding was later adopted by the GWR; alongside are some redundant spare corbels cut in 1903 for London Bridge, but never shipped.

5 *Follow the siding to the main line.*

C Another siding and an inclined plane appear ahead under Great King Tor.

6 *The siding is based on the P & DR main line near the GWR deviation and bridge over a moorland track. The GWR enters a cutting on the spur of King Tor; the P & DR is blocked by the GWR embankment and reappears beyond. Follow it.*

D The P & DR rounds the King Tor spur on a hillside ledge, where the view of the Walkham valley is very fine. On the grassy curve of the trackbed are three iron rail-chairs of 1823 still in position.

7 *The two lines unite beyond the cutting; follow the track to the Swell Tor-Foggin Tor col.*

E From Foggin Tor Quarry (left), came granite for Sir Thomas Tyrwhitt's Napoleonic war prison at Princetown.

8 *Follow the track until the prehistoric village (Note A) appears below (right).*

9 *Leave the track; keeping above the village, make for the Yestor valley.*

10 *Return to the start.*